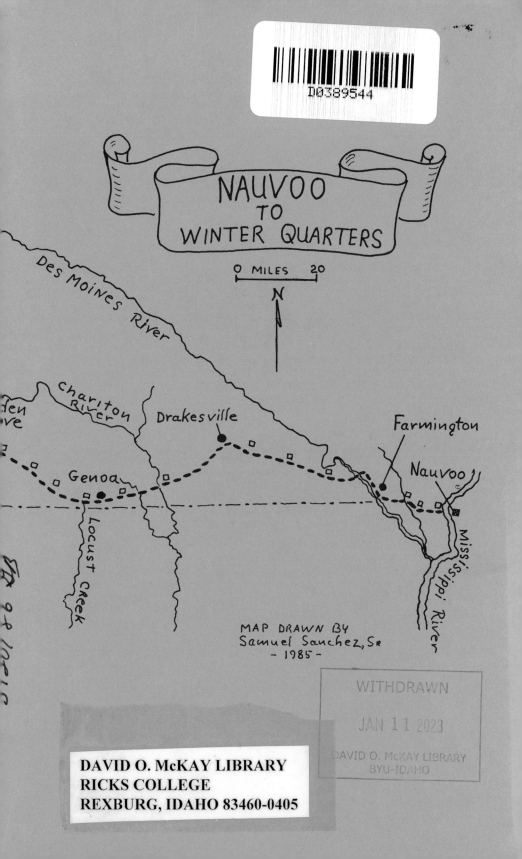

NAUVOO
TO
WINTER QUARTERS

0 MILES 20

N

Des Moines River

Chariton River

Drakesville

Farmington

Nauvoo

Genoa

Locust Creek

Mississippi River

MAP DRAWN BY
Samuel Sanchez, Sr
- 1985 -

WINTER QUARTERS

WINTER QUARTERS

CONREY BRYSON

Deseret Book Company
Salt Lake City, Utah

©1986 Deseret Book Company
All rights reserved
Printed in the United States of America

No part of this book may be reproduced in any form or by any
means without permission in writing from the publisher, Deseret
Book Company, P.O. Box 30178, Salt Lake City, Utah 84130

First printing April 1986

Library of Congress Cataloging-in-Publication Data

Bryson, Conrey.
  Winter quarters.

  Bibliography: p.
  Includes index.
  1. Mormons – Nebraska – Omaha – History – 19th century.
2. Omaha (Neb.) – History. I. Title.
F674.059M813 1986   978.2'254   86-2146
ISBN 0-87579-011-9

To the memory of my nine ancestors
who shared the Winter Quarters experience:
Amy Ward Hancock
Clarissa Hancock Alger
Samuel Alger
John Alger
Sarah Pulsipher Alger
Zera Pulsipher
Mary Brown Pulsipher
Margaret Cowan Bryson
Olivia Alger Bryson

CONTENTS

ACKNOWLEDGMENTS

Winter Quarters was born in a rare El Paso snowstorm. I picked up a copy of *American Heritage* and read an account of the Donner Party, nearly all of whom perished in the snow on their way to California in 1846. I reflected that a similar fate might have befallen the Mormon pioneers in that same year had it not been for Winter Quarters. It seemed to me that a book was called for on the subject of this vital way station for the migration westward.

While it was still snowing, I wrote Dr. Leonard Arrington, who was the Historian of The Church of Jesus Christ of Latter-day Saints, asking his advice about such a book. He was most encouraging and referred me to Dr. Glen M. Leonard, his assistant, who was equally encouraging. Dr. Leonard invited me to contact Jim Kimball, of the archives section of the Church History Department. Throughout the entire work, I have received both encouragement and assistance from these historians and members of their staffs. When I presented a paper entitled "Winter Quarters, More than a Valley Forge" at the 1983 Mormon History Association convention in Omaha, Dr. Arrington was present and renewed his encouragement.

In the course of research on this manuscript, I paid two visits to Omaha, especially to Florence, now a part of Omaha, and the site of Winter Quarters. There I was given a thorough tour of Mormon historical sites in the area by Gail George Holmes, local historian and former bishop of the Council Bluffs Ward. Bishop Holmes has rendered valuable assistance in the course of this work.

Attendants in the reference department of the Florence Branch, Omaha Public Library, were proud of their Winter Quarters collection and were eager to assist me in utilizing it. An active Florence Historical Society opened up the historical museum in the old

Florence National Bank building and displayed many important artifacts and records.

In El Paso, I received help and encouragement from many people. The reference department of the El Paso Public Library was always cooperative in helping me find important information. Mika Sharp helped to compile and type the appendix listing persons who died at Winter Quarters and Cutler's Park. Virginia Turner, of the *El Paso Herald Post*, was a source of continuing encouragement. Haywood Antone and Dale Walker, directors of Texas Western Press, my publisher on two previous books, were likewise sources of encouragement and advice. Then there was my constant mentor, dean of southwestern historians, Dr. C. L. Sonnichsen of Tucson, Arizona.

My son-in-law, Earl Hurst, introduced me to the journal of his great-grandfather Anson Call; President Gerald M. Pratt of the El Paso Mount Franklin Stake to the autobiography of his great-grandfather Parley P. Pratt; and Mrs. Wayne Graham to the journal of her ancestor William Clayton.

My wife and our extended family, her children and mine, were always encouraging. Fay accompanied me on all my research expeditions and always understood when my mind was 139 years and 1300 miles distant—in a place called Winter Quarters.

Come, come, ye Saints, no toil nor labor fear;
But with joy wend your way.
Though hard to you this journey may appear,
Grace shall be as your day.
'Tis better far for us to strive
Our useless cares from us to drive;
Do this, and joy your hearts will swell—
All is well! All is well!

Why should we mourn or think our lot is hard?
'Tis not so; all is right.
Why should we think to earn a great reward
If we now shun the fight?
Gird up your loins; fresh courage take.
Our God will never us forsake;
And soon we'll have this tale to tell—
All is well! All is well!

We'll find the place which God for us prepared,
Far away in the West,
Where none shall come to hurt or make afraid;
There the Saints will be blessed.
We'll make the air with music ring,
Shout praises to our God and King;
Above the rest these words we'll tell—
All is well! All is well!

And should we die before our journey's through,
Happy day! All is well!
We then are free from toil and sorrow, too;
With the just we shall dwell!
But if our lives are spared again
To see the Saints their rest obtain,
Oh, how we'll make this chorus swell—
All is well! All is well!

William Clayton

INTRODUCTION

At the northern fringes of the city of Omaha, Nebraska, Interstate 680 crosses the Missouri River on twin bridges. The bridge that carries the eastbound lanes has a large sign on it: MORMON BRIDGE.

The name "Mormon Bridge" came about after its groundbreaking ceremonies on May 12, 1951, at which Bishop LeGrand Richards, then Presiding Bishop of the Mormon church, was a principal speaker. At the ceremonies Dr. J. L. Karrer, of the North Omaha Bridge Commission, pointed out that the bridge was constructed on nearly the exact site of the old Mormon ferry, on which thousands of westbound immigrants crossed the Missouri from 1846 until the coming of the railroads in 1869. (At the ferry's eastern terminus, on the Iowa shore, there arose a prospering community known as Ferryville.)

The Mormon Bridge was completed in early 1953 and was dedicated during two days of ceremonies, May 31 and June 1.

This portion of Omaha was, until recent years, a small city known as Florence. Eventually the city of Omaha spread northward until it embraced the smaller community, and they became one city. But Florence still remembers its heritage, back to the days when it vied with Omaha for the route of the first transcontinental railroad, and back further still, when the site was the city of Winter Quarters, the first city in what later became the state of Nebraska.

Only a short distance south of the Mormon Bridge, just off Thirtieth Street, is the Florence branch of the Omaha Public Library. Here can be found a series of articles by local historian Gail George Holmes, a former bishop of the Council Bluffs Ward. His articles put Winter Quarters in perspective with the larger story

The Mormon Bridge spans the Missouri River near where the Saints crossed by ferry

of Mormon settlement, not only here, but at Council Bluffs and along the old Mormon trail back to Nauvoo as well.

Today Bishop Holmes is a valuable guide to the entire area. On my first visit to Omaha, he cheerfully gave an afternoon of his time to conduct me to points of interest on both sides of the Missouri River. He conducted me to the probable spot where the Camp of Israel first spread its tents on the Iowa side of the river, and where they were visited by a man who would be their valuable friend for the rest of his days, Colonel Thomas L. Kane. Colonel Kane's memorable description of the refugees at that site, given before the Pennsylvania Historical Society in 1850, became a much quoted appraisal of the character and courage of the Mormons. We visited Council Bluffs, which bore the name of Kanesville, in honor of Colonel Kane, and was home for the Latter-day Saints after Winter Quarters was vacated in 1848. There we saw the building where Orson Hyde, one of the Apostles who was left in charge at Kanesville, edited the *Frontier Guardian* for Latter-day Saints and others on their way westward.

Across the Missouri to the Nebraska side, we saw the site of Cold Spring Camp, one of the first stopping places for the Camp of Israel on the west bank. Some ten miles to the north and west, near a present day cemetery, we came to the site of Cutler's Park, named for Alpheus Cutler, faithful and valiant at this point in the migration. (Later, he became disaffected and led a small, rebellious group away from the Church he had served so well.) Near the cemetery is a cornfield that Bishop Holmes believes was the site of the cemetery at Cutler's Park. The miserable weather and meager, unbalanced diet during the long trip across Iowa took their toll and fifty-six graves were filled and marked at Cutler's Park before the move to Winter Quarters. No gravestones remain and no monument marks the place where these weary Mormons were laid to rest.

A short distance north of Cutler's Park, a modern highway leads back to the Mormon Bridge. Just south of it stands a building that is probably the only surviving building from the Winter Quarters era—the old mill. It has been greatly enlarged and altered during the past century but still contains the original structure. The Historical Landmark Council of the Florence Historical Foundation has erected a bronze marker that reads as follows:

The Florence Mill

The Florence Mill, one of the earliest in Nebraska, was constructed by the Mormons at Winter Quarters during the winter of 1846-47. Supplying both flour and lumber, the water-powered mill enabled the Mormons to cope more readily with the adverse conditions encountered during their stay in Nebraska. In 1847-48 groups of Mormons began to leave the area for the Salt Lake Valley, and as a result, Winter Quarters and the mill were abandoned.

In 1856, Alexander Hunter began to operate the mill. Its products helped fill the demands created by the growing town of Florence, established in 1854 on the old site of Winter Quarters.

By 1870, Jacob Weber had acquired the operation. Flour became its most important product, and by 1880, steam had largely replaced water as the motive force. The mill was further modified in later years to meet changing demands, and it continued to operate under the direction of second and third generation members of the Weber family.

Spanning more than a century, the history of the Florence Mill reflects the important contribution of the milling industry to the development of Nebraska.

There are many other memories of Winter Quarters in North Omaha today. The old Florence Bank, established in 1856 after the exodus from Winter Quarters and the birth of Florence, still stands as a museum. The museum preserves the old Florence telephone exchange, the living quarters of the bank's first president, and numerous historic pictures.

The principal thoroughfare, modern Thirtieth Street, approximates the course of Main Street in the original Winter Quarters.

Marker at the entrance to
the Mormon Pioneer
Cemetery

Just south of the bank, the city has preserved a public park, popularly known as Mormon Park, containing a historical marker with the words "Winter Quarters, location of the Camp of Israel," and "Pioneer Mormon Cemetery, one half of a mile west."

In 1936, this cemetery was purchased by The Church of Jesus Christ of Latter-day Saints and was dedicated by President Heber J. Grant on September 20, approximately the ninetieth anniversary of the Winter Quarters settlement.

The cemetery was closed to further burials in 1937, but in 1953 Oliver Fairbrass traveled to Utah to present his petition to Church authorities. Other members of the Fairbrass family had been buried in the historic ground before 1937, and he wanted his mother to be buried beside them. Permission was granted, and on April 28, 1953, Mrs. Bertha Fairbrass became the last burial in the Winter Quarters Cemetery.[1]

The Church has acquired a house across from the cemetery; it serves as a home for a missionary couple and as a visitor's center. Inside the gates is a monument whose centerpiece is an inspiring statue that was created by one of Utah's foremost sculptors, Avard Fairbanks. It portrays a man and a woman standing above the newly made grave of their child. Engraved on the monument is the closing stanza from William Clayton's great hymn of the Mormon migration, "Come, Come, Ye Saints":

And should we die before our journey's through,
Happy day! All is well!
We then are free from toil and sorrow, too;
With the just we shall dwell!

Also inscribed there is the following poem written by Florence Anderson for the dedication in 1936:

Driven away from old Nauvoo,
Three thousand Mormons rode
Across the plains to winter bed
In old Indian abode.
Housed in log cabins, camped in caves
In hillsides, huddled tight
In wagons, Mormons prayed and fought
The snow and freezing blight.
Ravaged by scurvy, cold, disease
And hunger, hundreds fell.
Their leader, Brigham Young held fast
His hand, they labored well,
But left in spring a grave-spread hill.
Upon its brow, now mild,
A man and a woman of bronze
Are burying their child.

In the background, a single memorial panel lists the names of more than three hundred people who were buried in the Winter

LDS Historical Church Archives

Monument at the cemetery depicting a pioneer couple who have just buried their child

Quarters Cemetery in the years 1846-48. Add to this fifty-six buried at Cutler's Park, and numerous others buried at Council Bluffs, Mount Pisgah, Garden Grove, Running Water, and at marked and unmarked graves across the Iowa and Nebraska plains, and the total approaches six hundred deaths in what may be called the Winter Quarters experience.[2]

The sacrifice in suffering and death at Winter Quarters is impressive and will be dealt with in a future chapter, but it is not the great message of Winter Quarters. The sacrifice was for a purpose, and at Winter Quarters that purpose was made firm.

At Winter Quarters the Saints burrowed in for the winter, most of them for two winters. As they learned sacrifice, they learned discipline and organization. They learned unity behind a great leader. When they established their refuge on the Missouri, Brigham Young was not the President of the Church; he was but President of the Quorum of the Twelve, and Winter Quarters was, especially for him, a time of testing. He and his followers learned to labor and to wait. They sang their songs, said their prayers, and danced their dances. They harvested crops, built wagons, and assembled provisions for themselves and for the thousands yet to come.

It was a motley gathering at Winter Quarters, and in the pages that follow we shall trace some of their origins, humble and great, as they heard the call "come to Zion." A bitter chapter will chronicle the triumph over mud, flood, and dissension as they moved across Iowa and managed to sing, "Why should we mourn or think our lot is hard? 'Tis not so; all is right." A chapter belongs to the municipal and ecclesiastic organization that truly made Winter Quarters a city. Equally deserving of a chapter in the chronicle is the careful preparation that made their destination more certain when their wagons moved westward in the spring of 1847.

A chapter describes some, among them some great leaders, who came to Winter Quarters, endured its hardships, and then decided to seek their fortune on the prairie soil rather than seek an unknown wilderness in the West. And a triumphant chapter belongs to the city that was reborn on the ruins of Winter Quarters and found a glorious heritage in the building of the West.

Before leaving Winter Quarters Cemetery, I paused to ponder the words of Hosea Stout. On the way to Winter Quarters, he had buried a wife and three children. Here on the banks of the Missouri,

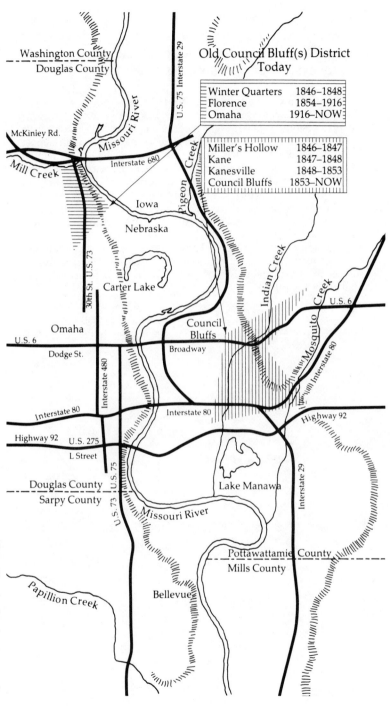

Old Council Bluff(s) District
Today

Winter Quarters	1846–1848
Florence	1854–1916
Omaha	1916–NOW

Miller's Hollow	1846–1847
Kane	1847–1848
Kanesville	1848–1853
Council Bluffs	1853–NOW

Washington County
Douglas County

Interstate 29

U.S. 75

Missouri River

McKinley Rd.

Mill Creek

Interstate 680

Pigeon Creek

Iowa

Nebraska

Carter Lake

30th St. U.S. 73

Omaha

U.S. 6

Dodge St.

Indian Creek

Council Bluffs

Broadway

Mosquito Creek

U.S. 6

Interstate 480

Interstate 80

Interstate 80

Interstate 80

Highway 92

Highway 92

U.S. 275

L Street

U.S. 75

Douglas County

Sarpy County

U.S. 73

Lake Manawa

Interstate 29

Missouri River

Pottawattamie County

Mills County

Papillion Creek

Bellevue

he moved the three remaining members of his family into a twelve-by-twelve log house. As yet, there were neither windows nor doors. Few of the cracks were stopped, and a chill north wind was blowing; but he still expressed his thanks. He wrote:

> Tonight, myself and family had the pleasure of once more sleeping in our own house, for the first time since we left Nauvoo on the 9th day of last February, making nine months and fifteen days that we have lived without a house during which time we have underwent almost every change of fortune that can be imagined. One half of my family, so dear to me, have been consigned to the silent grave and we who yet remain have often been brought to the verge of death. Often have I lain and contemplated my own sickness and feeble situation, without anything for myself and family to eat, with death staring me in the face, and could only contemplate what would become of them in case I was called away.
>
> But amid all these adverse changes, these heart-rending trials, not once yet have I ever regretted that I set out to follow the counsel of the people of God and to obey the voice of the Spirit to flee from the land of the Gentiles.[3]

Chapter One

A BEAUTIFUL AND DELIGHTFUL SITUATION

In September of 1846, the word Nebraska was but an ill-understood expression of the Omaha and Otoe Indians, perhaps derived from their name for the Platte River. Early explorers believed it was the name the Indians used to refer to the territory across the Missouri River westward from the bluffs on the Iowa side, where councils had been held among the various tribes and the westering Americans. It popularly bore the name of Council Bluffs.

During this time, many explorers crossed the wide Missouri near Council Bluffs. Peter Sarpy was holding together the promising community of Bellevue, down the river a few miles, by ferrying passengers to and from the bluffs, and by regaling Indians, trappers, military men, and explorers with his tales of adventure, triumph, and tragedy.[1]

But the community that formally came into being on September 23, 1846, was much more than a trading post or a casual location. It was the winter quarters of the Camp of Israel, and came to be named Winter Quarters. For the next two years, it would serve as the headquarters of one of the most significant migrations in American history. Then, after a brief hiatus that saw it sink into ruins, it would blossom again, under a new name, as that massive migration continued.

The founding of the city is signaled in the September 23 journal entry of Brigham Young, generally recognized as the leader of the Camp of Israel. He came to this uncertain position through his ordination as President of the Quorum of the Twelve Apostles, the governing body of The Church of Jesus Christ of Latter-day Saints, already popularly known as the Mormon church. Since the death of the Prophet and President, Joseph Smith, it had been

Brigham's position that the Presidency was dissolved and that the authority of leading the Church was vested in the Quorum of the Twelve. As the quorum's leader, he wrote in his journal: "The Camp of Israel began to move to the new location for Winter Quarters. The city was laid out in blocks of twenty rods by forty, each lot four rods by ten."[2]

Choosing the site was no hurried decision. Brigham Young knew full well that his authority to lead was challenged, within and without the Church, and he was careful to seek counsel before major decisions were made. Under the date of September 8, his journal recorded that a meeting of the High Council had named Alanson Eldredge, Alpheus Cutler, A. P. Rockwood, J. M. Grant, and Ezra Chase as the committee to locate Winter Quarters. It was planned early that it would be a place of some substance. On September 9, Brigham recorded that twelve teams were ready to leave for Nauvoo to bring the poor and others still remaining in and around that beleaguered city to the new settlement on the Missouri. Elder Orson Hyde reported that sixty-four families in St. Louis were ready to emigrate westward if teams could be sent to them, and eighty-two others intended to emigrate as soon as they could obtain the necessary means. The proper location of a winter quarters was gaining importance, and Brigham Young summarized the situation for the High Council. He said:

> I said my feelings were at present to stay here and locate our families for a year or two; meanwhile fit out companies to go over the mountains with seed grain, mille, etc. to sow, prepare and build for our families that we need not carry provisions for them over the mountains, and wished the committee to have this in view in settling this camp, and select healthy locations.[3]

On September 10, the committee on locations was ready with its report. It recommended that the settlement be located on both sides of Willow Creek, northeast of the encampment at Cutler's Park, which was the central location of the migrating Saints. On Friday, September 11, Brigham Young wrote: "About half past ten A.M., Elders Heber C. Kimball, Orson Pratt, Willard Richards, Wilford Woodruff, George A. Smith, Amasa Lyman, and I walked northwards and selected the site for winter quarters and returned to camp. After dinner, accompanied by the High Council and Marshall, we returned and I commenced the survey."

Brigham Young already had experience in surveying a city. He was a close confidante of President Joseph Smith in 1833 when President Smith announced a revelation on the building of a City of Zion. Primarily, the plan was for the building of a new city on the western edge of Missouri, the present site of Independence; but, as the Prophet sent his plans from Kirtland, Ohio, to his brethren in Missouri, he was thinking of many planned communities to be built in the future. This is evident when he said, "Lay off another in the same way and so fill up the world in these last days."[4]

That first City of Zion was hardly begun when its builders were driven from Jackson County, but the idea of building such a city still lived and was cultivated. The next site was the city of Far West, in Caldwell County, where a site was carefully surveyed, streets were laid out, and ground was broken for what was to be a holy temple. Here, too, the Saints were driven out by mobs, and at nearby Haun's Mill seventeen were massacred. They tried also in Davies County at a place called Adam-Ondi-Ahman, but the work of the settlement had hardly begun when Governor Lilburn W. Boggs issued an order that the Mormons must be driven from the state or exterminated.

The Church's next attempt at building a city was highly successful. The refugees from Missouri, with an increasing number of converts from the United States and Europe, reclaimed a swampy, unhealthful area on the banks of the Mississippi in Illinois and called it Nauvoo, translated by Joseph Smith as "the city beautiful." Nauvoo was large enough that its active, voting citizens became a source of coveted political power. At first welcomed, the Mormons later became involved with bitter controversies, both with older Illinois residents and with apostate factions within their own church. These conflicts resulted in a mob killing President Joseph Smith and his brother Hyrum, while they were confined in a jail at Carthage, Illinois, awaiting trial.

Again the Mormons found it necessary to abandon their City of Zion, and under the leadership of Brigham Young, they undertook a mass migration toward an unknown destination in the Rocky Mountains. The Missouri River marked the end of their migration in 1846, and there they set up their winter quarters to await the coming of spring and the renewal of their pilgrimage to yet another Zion. In planning the city of Winter Quarters, Brigham Young felt the sacred obligation to build a true City of Zion, no matter how temporary. He began by laying out Main Street, with the other streets running parallel or perpendicular to it. The blocks were laid off before any of the houses were built and were named for important people in the Church.[5]

This new city might be said to have had an extensive set of suburbs. Twice on the journey across Iowa, the Mormons stopped to build communities and plant crops for the sustenance of thousands to follow. These Iowa satellite communities were known as Garden Grove and Mount Pisgah. (The latter was named by Parley Pratt, one of the Church's greatest missionaries and a member of the Quorum of the Twelve. Gazing westward from one of the higher elevations on the flat plains of Iowa, Parley said he knew how Moses felt as he gazed into the promised land atop Mount Pisgah.[6])

Then, although the headquarters of the Church had moved to Winter Quarters, there were still Latter-day Saints in the Council Bluffs area to the east. And about 150 miles west of Winter Quarters, where a stream known as Running Water entered the Platte, yet another suburb was built. Bishop George Miller, Anson Call, and Joseph Holbrook were among those who had outdistanced Brigham Young and were headed for the mountains. They were counseled, instead, to go no further westward that season and proceeded to build a fort and wait for springtime.[7]

Each of these settlements, although suburban to Winter Quarters, received all communications intended for "Camp of Israel, Winter Quarters" during the ensuing winter. They were definitely part of the Winter Quarters experience.

Hosea Stout, Winter Quarters' chief of police, had been a member of the Nauvoo Legion and chief of the Nauvoo police in the perilous days when the Saints were preparing to vacate. He had been one of the bodyguards to Brigham Young and the Quorum of the Twelve along the trek across Iowa. Along the way, he had buried three of his children in hurriedly marked graves. At long last, he could contemplate a relatively permanent dwelling place, if only for a season. In his journal, he described his first impressions of Winter Quarters. He wrote:

> Foggy morning. Camp still moving. I went down to the new location today to make a location for the 4th sub-division of the first grand division of the Camp of Israel. I located a place near the center of the

city. It consisted of one block containing twenty lots. The City, for so it was laid out, was situated on a level plat on the second bluff from the river, and about 50 or 60 feet above the water, and was quite narrow at the north end of the City, the third bluff coming near to the river. As you go south, the river seems to retreat from this bluff, leaving this flat or city ground wider as you go south. The City is now one mile from south to north, and bounded at each end by two brooks of good running water. The north brook is calculated to have a mill built on it, with some 20 feet or more of fall.

When I first came into the place, I saw Brigham, who showed me the plan he had for the defense of the place and the three points where he intended to put the artillery which would effectively protect the whole place. This was a beautiful and delightful situation for a City, and I was pleased with this my first view of it.

Two days after he had written this glowing description, and before he could move his family into Winter Quarters, he was burying his lovely twenty-year-old wife, Marinda. She had accepted the doctrine of plural marriage. She had followed her husband with faith and courage through all the trials across Iowa; and west of the Missouri, she died of childbirth — she and her babe.

The best-known midwife of Israel, Patty Bartlett Sessions, was not present to attend Marinda, for here at Cutler's Park she came near to filling her own spot in the growing Cutler's Park cemetery. In early September, Patty wrote in her diary:

> I have been very sick and have not wrote any since the 7th of August. . . . I did not have my clothes on for 20 days. I vomited 9 days and nights. Got to the camp on Tuesday. Brother Brigham and Heber laid hands on me. Sister Young gave me some tonic on Wednesday that seemed to reach my disease. The doctor said I had inflammation of the stomach and it would be a miracle if I got well.
>
> When they told me I was almost gone, I felt calm and composed, told them where my garments were and all the things necessary for my burial, and requested to have the latitude and longitude taken where I was lain and also to have cedar posts put down to my grave, with my name cut on them, so that I could be found when called for. Many thought I was dying, and the news went out that I was dead. But the saints held on to me by faith and prayer, and through their faith and the power of the Priesthood, I was healed.[8]

The people who were moving into Winter Quarters that September were not the usual run of westering Americans in 1846. Colonel Thomas L. Kane first encountered this unique people when he came upon the Camp of Israel on the east bank of the Missouri, before they traveled to their winter quarters. Four years later, he gave his appraisal of these emigrants in a memorable address to the Historical Society of Pennsylvania. He said:

> This landing and the large flat or bottoms on the east side of the river were crowded with covered carts and wagons, and each one of the Council Bluff hills was crowded with its own great camp, gay with bright white canvas and alive with the busy stir of swarming occupants. In the clear blue morning air, the smoke steamed up from more than a thousand cooking fires. Countless roads and bypaths checkered all manner of geometric figures on the hillsides.
>
> Herd boys were dozing upon the slopes; sheep and horses, cows and oxen, were feeding around them and other herds in the luxuriant meadow of the then swollen river. From a single point, I counted four thousand head of cattle in view at one time. As I approached the camp, it seemed to me that the children there were to prove still more numerous. Along the little creek I had to cross were women in greater force than the *blanchisseuses* upon the Seine, washing and rinsing all manner of white muslins, red flannels, and parti-colored calicos, and hanging them to bleach upon a greater area of grass and bushes than we can display in all our Washington Square.
>
> Hastening by these, I saluted a group of noisy boys, whose purely vernacular cries had for me an invincible home-savoring attraction. It was one of them, a bright faced lad, who, hurrying on his jacket and trousers, fresh from bathing in the creek, first assured me I was at my right destination. He was a mere child, but he told me of his own accord where I had best go to seek my welcome, and took my horse's bridle to help me pass a morass, the bridge of which he alleged to be unsafe.
>
> There was something joyous for me in my free rambles about this vast body of pilgrims. I could range all the wild country wherever I liked, under safeguard of their moving host. Not only in the main camps was all stir and life, but in every direction it seemed to me I could follow "Mormon roads," and find them beaten and hard and even dusty by the wear and tread of the cattle and vehicles of emigrants laboring over them. By day I would overtake and pass one after another, what amounted to an army train of them, and at night, if I encamped where the timber and running water were found together, I was almost sure to be within call of some camp or other, or at least within sight of its watch fires. Wherever I was compelled to tarry, I was certain to find hospitality, scant indeed, but never stinted and always honest and kind.
>
> After a recent unavoidable association with the border inhabitants of western Missouri and Iowa, the vile scum which our own society, to apply the words of an admirable gentleman and eminent divine, Rev. Dr. Morton of Philadelphia, "like the great ocean washes upon its frontier shores," I can scarcely describe the gratification I felt in associating with persons who were almost all of eastern American origin—persons of refined and cleanly habits and decent language, and in observing their peculiar and interesting mode of life; while every day seemed to bring its own special incident, fruitful in the illustration of habits and character.[9]

Even allowing for Colonel Kane's prejudices in favor of his own part of America, and the warm affection that Mormon hospitality had created, the people who came at long last to Winter Quarters were a special people, bound together by ties of faith that surmounted tribulation and death, and softened and gentled by principles taught on every Sabbath in the midst of their afflictions, then reinforced by prayers around the campfires and in their wagons.

They were a select people, selected from out of the world to hear the call of "come to Zion," even if Zion should be but a temporary stopping place beyond the Missouri.

Chapter Two

COME TO ZION

Richard Smyth wrote the stirring hymn "Israel, Israel, God Is Calling," which became a rallying call to thousands who decided to flee from "lands of woe."[1]

> Israel, Israel, God is calling,
> Calling thee from lands of woe.
> Babylon the great is falling;
> God shall all her towers o'erthrow.
> Come to Zion, Come to Zion
> Ere his floods of anger flow.
> Come to Zion, Come to Zion
> Ere his floods of anger flow.

Long before Richard Smyth put the call into such challenging words, thoughtful men were thinking similar thoughts. As the third decade of the nineteenth century began, many Americans pondered the reasons for the creation of their country that was beckoning people to come from all the world. Was this something more than just a noble political experiment? Did God actually have in mind that in the freedom of this new land, his true gospel would flourish best? Was this the "dispensation of the fulness of times" as proclaimed in the scriptures?

Among the Saints streaming into Winter Quarters in late 1846, there were many who had searched the scriptures and heard the strange whisperings. Some had pondered Joel 2:28, 30: "Your old men shall dream dreams, your young men shall see visions: And I will shew wonders in the heavens and in the earth."

In upstate New York in the year 1827, there were many who searched the heavens. The northern lights had been especially visible in the northern latitude that year, and many watched them and pondered. In the little town of Mendon, New York, a young man named Heber C. Kimball witnessed a heavenly display that defied all description. He carried to his neighbor Brigham Young the news of the strange phenomenon. A few years later, Brigham shared with him a book that had been left in the neighborhood by a traveling missionary. It was called the Book of Mormon.

Before they had ever met the Prophet, who could tell them of the book's divine origin, they knew that the everlasting gospel had been restored. Together, in December 1832, with Brigham's wife, brother, and sister-in-law, they drove a sleigh over snow-capped roads to Columbia, Pennsylvania, to find the nearest branch of The Church of Jesus Christ of Latter-day Saints and to request baptism.

To some, the call to Zion came, not in dramatic heavenly manifestations, but in quiet whisperings of the Spirit. What was the powerful whispering that caused Parley Parker Pratt, one day in 1830, to suddenly leave the canal boat in which he and his wife were traveling back to their home in eastern New York, assure her he would complete the journey later on, and then embark on a quest for truth that led him to the Prophet Joseph Smith? He found the truth and became one of the most ardent missionaries the Church has ever known.

In 1836, a knock came upon the door of Parley P. Pratt's house after he had retired for the night. The caller was Heber C. Kimball, a fellow member of the Quorum of the Twelve. Heber had come to call Parley to one of the most fruitful missions of his life. He was directed to go to the city of Toronto, Canada, and organize a branch of the Church there. He was promised that "from the things growing out of this mission shall the fullness of the gospel spread into England, and cause a great work to be done in that land."[2]

Few prophecies were fulfilled more forcefully. In Toronto, Parley encountered a Methodist study group that was holding private meetings to seek out the truths of the gospel of Jesus Christ. From the group came John Taylor, future President of the Church; his wife, Leonora Cannon Taylor; Theodore Turley; Joseph Fielding and his sisters, Mary and Mercy; Isaac Russell; John Goodson; Stephen Hales; and others. As prophesied, among these were the first missionaries to go to England when the gospel was introduced there in 1837. The gospel did indeed spread like wildfire and bring to Zion thousands who felt they were truly being called "from lands of woe." Many of them were in the throngs that poured into Winter Quarters in 1846. They had heard and followed the call to come to Zion, whether it be Kirtland, Far West, Nauvoo, or across the wide Missouri.

One who heard the call was Margaret Cowan Bryson, a widow who lived in Banbridge, County Down, Ireland. Her husband, John Bryson, had never returned following the Napoléonic Wars and was last heard of in a veteran's home in London in 1825. He never saw his son, Samuel, born in 1815. When Samuel was 17, he enlisted in the British Army and served for some seven years. After many prayers for his safe return, Margaret had a dream in which she clutched a single butterfly to her bosom. From the one butterfly came two, and from the two came many more. She felt certain that her son would return safely and would have many offspring.

Margaret had another dream. She dreamed that two men came to Banbridge bringing a new religion and that she accepted it. When the first Latter-day Saint missionaries came to town, she eagerly accepted the restored gospel, as did her son and daughter-in-law.

The call of "come to Zion" was irresistible to her. She saved every penny and finally borrowed money from another convert, John Hamilton, to pay her passage across the Atlantic to Nauvoo. She was among 180 immigrants on the *Swanton*, a Church-chartered vessel that sailed from Liverpool on January 16, 1843. At New Orleans, the passengers on the *Swanton* transferred to the riverboat *Amaranth* and arrived in Nauvoo on April 12. The passengers were met at the dock and welcomed to Zion by the Prophet Joseph Smith himself. They were also welcomed by the Prophet's brother Hyrum, who was the Patriarch of the Church. The hospitable Hyrum, always eager to help new converts adjust to life in a new world, offered Margaret employment in his own home to help pay for her passage.[3]

The *Amaranth* was the first of two vessels filled with converts to dock at Nauvoo on April 12. At five o'clock that same afternoon, the *Maid of Iowa*, came into the docks bearing another 200 converts under the direction of Parley P. Pratt. How many of these 540 new residents of Nauvoo found shelter in the Hyrum Smith household is not known, but Hyrum's great-grandson records that "Hyrum's household included as many as twelve to twenty in all. Out of pity, the Patriarch continually housed and fed certain elderly and unemployable persons."[4]

When Margaret Bryson moved into the Smith household,

events that were to drive the Saints from Nauvoo were already beginning to take shape. Joseph Smith was continually threatened with arrests stemming from troubles in Missouri. Some of his most trusted lieutenants in the building up of Nauvoo had apostatized from the Church and had become his mortal enemies. One court appearance after another finally terminated in the confining of Joseph, Hyrum, and other Church leaders in a tiny jail in Carthage, Illinois, in June of 1844. On June 27, both Joseph and Hyrum were killed by a mob.

Anyone who dreamed that the death of its Prophet would destroy the Church failed to count on the preparations the Prophet and his associates had made for such an eventuality. A plan of organization under which the governing of the Church would devolve from the Presidency to the Quorum of the Twelve was placed into effect. Brigham Young, as President of that Quorum, became acting President of the Church. Hope that the Church could survive and prosper in Nauvoo may have been dim, but that it would prosper, somewhere, the faithful did not doubt. Most of the Church leaders would concur with the prophetic words of Apostle Orson Hyde, delivered in Boston, on July 18, 1844. He said:

> I will prophesy that, instead of the work dying, it will be like the mustard stock that was ripe, that a man undertook to throw out of his garden, and scattered seed all over it, and next year it was nothing but mustard. It will be so by shedding the blood of the prophets — it will make ten Saints where there is but one now.[5]

Orson Hyde's bold prophecy was already in the process of fulfillment. In the early months of 1844, 501 converts had sailed on four chartered vessels from Liverpool and landed at New Orleans. The last of these reached Nauvoo a few days before the martyrdom. On September 17, 143 converts, aware of the death of their prophet, nevertheless heeded the call of "come to Zion" and sailed from Liverpool on the sailing vessel *Norfolk*.[6]

As Acting President of the Church, Brigham Young continued to urge the building up of Nauvoo and the completion of its temple, but even as the frantic efforts to complete the temple moved forward, there was one threat after another of mob action by enemies of the Church. In January of 1845, a bill was introduced in the Illinois legislature to revoke the charter of the City of Nauvoo. Even while Church members and their friends were working against the passage of this bill, plans were being considered for a possible refuge in the far west. On January 7, the Quorum of the Twelve met in the uncompleted temple and discussed "the subject of sending a company to California . . . ; also the propriety of sending to the branches of the Church abroad for teams to help the expedition." Before the month was out, the charter was repealed.

On April 8, 1845, Governor Thomas Ford of Illinois wrote a letter evidently intended to be helpful, but it could in no way be considered as an invitation to remain in Illinois: "In case a mob should be raised against you, it will be your privilege and one of your highest duties to society to resist it. But you know your condition as a people. You know the prejudices which exist and the disposition of the public mind to believe evil of you. You will therefore have to be cautious."

The governor closed his long letter with a suggestion. "California," he said, "now offers a field for the prettiest enterprise that has been undertaken in modern times. . . . Why would it not be a pretty operation for your people to go out there, take possession of and conquer a portion of the vacant country, and establish an independent government of your own, subject only to the laws of nations?"[7]

— The governor's undiplomatic observations might serve future generations as proof of the United States' intentions to steal by force a large slice of Mexico territory; but to the Mormons at Nauvoo it could only serve as a warning that they could not remain long in Illinois for the government would be unable to protect them. This warning was reinforced with violence the following September, when mobs attacked the settlements of Lima and Morley, some twenty miles southwest of Nauvoo. The mobs burned many of the Saints' houses and sent them streaming into Nauvoo for refuge. Brigham Young ordered every man who had a team in the area to help with the evacuation.[8]

From that day forward, almost every day in Brigham Young's record tells of further preparations for the general departure for the West. No date was set, but the words "next spring" appear again and again. With the coming of the new year, 1846, the attention of the Saints was centered on the completion of their temple so holy ordinances could be administered to bless them as they started into the unknown. On January 1, although plasterers were still finishing the interior, it was felt that the giving of endowments should begin. Eighty-nine persons received their endowments on that New Year's Day, 64 the following day, 114 on the third, 104 on the fourth; and so it continued day after day.[9]

On January 13, 140 horses and 70 wagons were reported ready for immediate service in the westward movement. Following a pattern set for the migration of ancient Israel from Egypt to the promised land, the Saints organized into companies of tens, fifties, and hundreds, with a captain over each.[10] Wagons ready, their temple endowments completed, and threats of mob action mounting, many of the Saints could not wait until spring to leave. On February 4, Charles Shumway became the first to cross the Mississippi, his wagon on a skiff, moving through the ice floes that nearly clogged the river. Two days later, six wagons under the direction of Bishop George Miller crossed. The great migration was under way, and its constant stream would continue for months and years.

Mary Fielding Smith, Hyrum's widow, waited to leave Nauvoo. She had to sell her property and care for the sick and poor left behind. Her brother, Joseph Fielding, and his wife camped with her while she was delayed. In early September, some five hundred men gathered at Carthage and began an invasion of Nauvoo. Mary accepted the best available offer for her property, and as the battle of Nauvoo was under way, the Fielding company crossed the Mississippi in nine wagons and began their journey across Iowa.[11]

The Fielding group joined a large number of Saints driven from Nauvoo and camped on the west bank of the Mississippi. On September 9, as Brigham Young and his aides were preparing the move into the settlement they would call Winter Quarters, they dispatched twelve teams and wagons toward Nauvoo to help those left behind—especially the widow of the fallen Patriarch. An additional group of teamsters was recruited to drive to St. Louis, there to help sixty-four families ready to start toward Winter Quarters.[12]

Included in the shivering camp of the poor and sick was Thomas Bullock, who was secretary to the Prophet Joseph at the time of his martyrdom. In the spring of 1846, sickness overtook him and his family. He spent the long summer fighting illness and poverty. In late September, when ravaging mobs drove the last of the Mormons from Nauvoo, he was suffering from chills and fever as he made camp west of the Mississippi.

His journal of September 23, 1846, is a vivid description of life among the last refugees from Nauvoo. He wrote:

> About noon, a tremendous thunderstorm passed over our camp. The rain poured down in torrents and swept under the tents; it poured through my wagon cover. The carpet was one complete pool. Although in a raging fever, I had to ladle the water out with a basin, while my wife sat up, catching the water with a washbowl and dishes. All the beds, bedding and clothing got thoroughly drenched.
>
> There were several other storms during the evening and night, which kept us miserable in our wet beds, not having one dry thread on. One poor woman took off her petticoat, having cast it around her four children, and then kept huddled together. Seven or eight poor, shaking creatures, others burning with fever, went to one tent, crammed themselves in; others crept under wagons and bushes. A more doleful day and night was seldom if ever equaled.

There was more suffering and several deaths before this last company of refugees from Nauvoo made their way across the mud-soaked plains of Iowa. The first snow of the season had blanketed the plains on November 28 when they crossed the Missouri into Winter Quarters. Thomas Bullock went at once to a meeting of Brigham Young and the Municipal High Council and took the minutes of its proceedings.

On December 17, he walked the streets of Winter Quarters, estimated the population at four thousand, and drew a map of the settlement. In his journal, he recorded: "I went through the city where nine weeks before there was not a footpath nor a cowpath, but now may be seen hundreds of houses, and hundreds more in different stages of completion, impossible to distinguish the rich from the poor, the streets are wide and regular and every prospect of a large city being raised up here."[13]

With his health improving and his own modest home under construction, Thomas Bullock was content in this Zion in the wilderness.

Chapter Three

WHY SHOULD WE MOURN?

For seventeen-year-old Helen Mar Kimball Whitney, the trek across Iowa began as a honeymoon. In early 1846, she was very much in love with Horace K. Whitney. At twilight on February 3, a messenger brought them word that the work on the Nauvoo Temple was complete enough that they might present themselves that evening. Remembering the event, she wrote:

> The weather being fine, we preferred to walk; and as we passed through the little graveyard at the foot of the hill, a solemn covenant we entered into—to cling to each other through time, and if permitted, through all eternity, and this was solemnized at the holy altar.
>
> We are going out from the world to live beyond the Rocky Mountains, where none other will wish to go, and we are never again to mingle with Babylon, but remain a distinct and separate people.

The wedding reception lasted until midnight, probably in the Nauvoo Temple, for Brigham Young had given permission for dancing there prior to its dedication. After the music ceased, Helen's father, Heber C. Kimball, approached her. He was carrying a box, which he handed to her, and said, "Now Helen, go to and pack up your things."

The packing and preparations were not easy and were beset with many troubles. Helen recalled the troubles years later, and she wrote:

> Being short of wagons and teams, in order to lighten the load, we carried our change of apparel in bags made convenient for that purpose. We were assisted in our sewing by two or more of father's wives, as there were clothes to make for the boys, and a great deal to do and a short time to do it in.
>
> Mother's health was then feeble, and she had three little boys with the whooping cough. The babe was thirteen months old, who, as soon as he commenced coughing, would lose his breath, and we would have to toss him out into the cold air, which seemed the only thing to bring

him to. Bishop Whitney's family and a great many more were in a
similar or worse condition, but when they heard the cry "to your tents,
oh Israel," they left their comfortable homes and the graves of their
loved ones, and followed the voice of the one whom they knew the
Lord had chosen to lead his people.

It was February 16 when Heber C. Kimball's large family crossed
the Mississippi. Brigham Young's family and a great many others
had crossed a day earlier, and a large community of Saints had set
up a temporary gathering place at Sugar Creek, nine miles west
of Nauvoo. The exodus was being made through snow and mud.
Helen was riding a pony, and when she passed the wagons of
William Taylor, Joseph Knight, and Richard Ballantyne, she was
so cold and weary she could no longer ride. They stopped, made
a fire on the prairie, gave Helen warmth and a little wine, and the
entire group came into Sugar Creek about seven o'clock in the
evening; their first day of a journey of more than a thousand miles,
and they had traveled but nine.

At Sugar Creek the snow was so deep that paths had to be
shoveled among the tents and wagons. The Sugar Creek camp had
been selected because of available timber, and soon roaring fires
were blazing throughout the camp. Heber C. Kimball had pitched
a tent with a sheet iron stove at one end, and Helen recorded,
"When we had warmed ourselves, we made our beds upon the
ground, and laid down with grateful hearts for a comfortable shelter, and slept soundly till morning."[1]

Life at Sugar Creek had already begun to pall upon people who
were anxious to move on westward. Some had been there two
weeks. Tempers were beginning to flare, and Saints were beginning to stray, as indicated in the journal of President Young on
February 17. He wrote:

> All the brethren of the Camp assembled near the bridge, when I
> arose in a wagon and cried with a loud voice, "Attention, the whole
> camp of Israel!" I proceeded to explain the cause of delay of the camp,
> which was in short that Bishop Whitney and Elders H. C. Kimball and
> William Clayton were not ready, or were waiting to secure and bring
> with them Church property needed in the camp. Some of the brethren
> have been here nearly two weeks, and if all had come according to
> counsel, I should have been here much sooner, if I had come without
> a shirt to my back.
> I wish the brethren to stop running to Nauvoo, hunting, fishing,
> and roasting their shins, idling away their time, and fix nosebaskets for
> their horses, and save their corn, and fix comfortable places for their

wives and children to ride, and never borrow without asking leave, and be sure and return what was borrowed lest your brother be vexed with you and in his anger, curse you. That all dogs in the camp should be killed, if the owners would not tie them up, and any man who would keep a horse in camp that had the horse distemper ought to forfeit all his horses.

We will have no laws we cannot keep, but we will have order in the camp. If any want to live in peace when we have left this, they must toe the mark.

I then called upon all who wanted to go with the camp to raise their right hands, and all hands went up.[2]

They wanted to go, but it would be many days yet before the Camp of Israel was under way. William Clayton was still in Nauvoo. He was no frontiersman; his background was clerical. He was an important secretary to Joseph Smith, and then to Brigham Young. When Brigham Young's group crossed the river, William was worried about his young wife, Diantha, who was expecting their first child at any time. Reluctantly, he decided to leave her in Nauvoo and prepare to cross the river. Her father's family would care for her until William should send for her.

Important records and other Church properties were left in William Clayton's care; he recorded that on February 13, he sent four loads of goods across the river and was busy loading and packing. On February 15, two teams were sent across and on February 16 and 17, he was "still loading teams." On February 18, Brigham Young, Heber C. Kimball, and J. M. Grant were among those who went to William Clayton's group to hurry them. The next day, William recorded: "This morning the ground is covered with snow. It is so windy they cannot cross the river. Continued to snow all day."[3]

At the camp on Sugar Creek, conditions were even worse. Willard Richards made these entries in the camp journal:

> The wind blew steadily from the northwest, accompanied by snow which fell to the depth of seven or eight inches, but which thawed as it fell. The storm was unceasing, and the evening was very cold, which caused much suffering in the camp, for there were many who had no tents or any comfortable place to lodge; many tents were blown down. Some of them were unfinished and had no ends.
>
> Friday, February 20. Extremely cold, considerable ice floating in the Mississippi.
>
> About fifteen hundred bushels of tithing corn which had previously been gathered up in Lee County, together with a large amount of potatoes, turnips, and other grains and vegetables had been mostly consumed by the camp. The cold increased throughout the day, the

night was very severe; at many points ice was fastened on the banks
of the river.
    Saturday, February 21. Cold continues. Elders Orson Pratt, Amasa
Lyman, George A. Smith, George Miller and Albert Rockwood in Council in the Historian's tent.

This emergency meeting of the Council, in the absence of
Brigham Young and Heber C. Kimball, was called to deal with
freezing conditions and possible starvation. An emergency purchase of five hundred bushels of corn, together with hay and straw,
was authorized. Captain Stephen Markham was asked to have all
the tithing wheat and rye ground and to report to the Council.
Individuals possessing surplus amounts of grain were to have it
ground into flour and stored for future use. Though faced with all
their trials, Willard Richards reported that "the Saints in camp
were patient, and endured all their privations without murmur-
ing."
    The next day, ice was flowing so swiftly in the river that
President Young, Heber C. Kimball, and John Taylor were able to
cross only in a skiff, which darted with great danger among the
sharp ice floes. At seven o'clock, February 22, they were reunited
with the camp at Sugar Creek.[4]
    William Clayton had found it impossible to follow his leaders
in their dangerous crossing of the Mississippi. He waited another
five days for favorable weather before crossing. It was four o'clock
on February 27 when he arrived. One of his first and most eagerly
awaited acts was to take his place in the band, conducted by Captain William Pitt. On the last day of February, the band played a
welcome for Bishop Newel K. Whitney. With his arrival, the Camp
of Israel seemed complete enough to resume its journey.[5]
    At six o'clock on the morning of March 1, four hundred wagons,
with a population of some five hundred persons, were on their
way. The temperature was recorded at nineteen degrees above zero,
but the skies were fair as the wagons began to move. These were
not seasoned travelers. Many were sick. Some were bitter at the
delays that had kept them at Sugar Creek for nearly a month. Now,
delays were continuing, and by ten o'clock many of the wagons
were still not ready to move. At ten thirty, Heber C. Kimball called
the camp together and announced that President Young, suffering
from rheumatism, could not speak to them. Then Heber proceeded

to speak to the camp. Brigham Young recorded parts of Heber's message when he wrote:

> I wished him to say to the Saints that it was my will for the camp to move to some other location, because while we are so near Nauvoo, the brethren are continually going back and neglecting their teams and families, and running to me for counsel about a little property they may have, here or there or somewhere.
>
> President Kimball said no doubt many would be tried, and he would see the kingdom of God established and all the kingdoms of this world become the kingdom of God and his Christ—[he] referred to his travels in Missouri—[he] encouraged the brethren to go forward, and felt that the grass would start before long, [and] that we were not going out of this world.... He then called upon all who meant to go ahead to say "I," which was responded to heartily by the brethren present. No doubt you mean to have President Young for your leader. We will do all that he says and everything will be all right.[6]

The last words quoted may be some indication of the slender thread that held Brigham Young to the leadership of the Camp of Israel. The principle, now well established in the Church, that the President of the Quorum of the Twelve Apostles assumes leadership when the First Presidency is dissolved, was by no means certain in 1846. Many times Brigham sought to confirm his leadership by vote of the people. He was not yet President of the Church, only of the Quorum of the Twelve.

Despite his rheumatism, he called the Camp of Israel into full motion by noon. Brigham himself waited for the arrival of his carriage from Nauvoo, and it was sunset before he was under way. Going down the hill toward their next encampment, his carriage came near to being upset and was saved only through the work of Jesse D. Hunter. Parley P. Pratt's wagon, moving down that same hill, suffered greater misfortune. The neck yoke broke, and oxen and wagon were scattered among the tents and women and children below, but no one was injured. The camp had moved only five miles and was still along the banks of Sugar Creek, a scant fourteen miles from Nauvoo. The problem of feeding the multitude continued, but some of the pioneers who had moved ahead to blaze the trail had taken a job of cutting and splitting three thousand rails and husking one hundred and fifty shocks of corn, which supplied the camp with both corn and fodder.

With the very real threat of violence from enemies of the Church in both Missouri and Illinois, a safe passage across Iowa

was essential. Thus, Brigham penned a letter to the governor of
Iowa:

> To His Excellency
> Governor of the Territory of Iowa,
> Honored Sir:
> The time is at hand in which several thousand free citizens of this
> great Republic are to be driven from their peaceful homes and firesides;
> their property and their dearest constitutional rights, to wander in the
> barren plains and sterile mountains of the western wilds, and linger
> out their lives in wretched exile far beyond the pale of professed civili-
> zation, or else be exterminated upon their own lands by the people and
> authorities of the State of Illinois. As life is sweet, we have chosen
> banishment rather than death. . . .
> Therefore, we the presiding authorities of the Church of Jesus
> Christ of Latter-day Saints, as a committee on behalf of several thousand
> suffering exiles, humbly ask your excellency to protect us in our con-
> stitutional rights while we are passing through the territory over which
> you have jurisdiction. And should any of the exiles be under the neces-
> sity of stopping in this Territory for a time, either in the settled or
> unsettled parts, for the purpose of raising crops, by renting farms, or
> upon the public lands or to make the preparations for their exile in any
> lawful way, we humbly petition your Excellency to use an influence
> and power in our behalf; and thus preserve thousands of American
> citizens, together with their wives and children from intense sufferings,
> starvation and death.
> And, your petitioners will ever pray.[7]

More than a century later, this plea to the governor seems
melodramatic. However, in the context of the suffering already
experienced by these exiles, it is more realistic. The Mormons saw
the good will and assistance of the government and people of Iowa
as their best immediate hope for relief from their troubles.

It was September before a reply was received from the governor,
and by then the first group of pioneers had already crossed the
Missouri into Nebraska. But the letter was not needed; there was
no persecution by the government or people of Iowa. On the con-
trary, they gave much assistance.

On March 2, the thermometer stood at twenty-three degrees,
and the skies were clear. The camp began moving at nine o'clock
in the morning, and the roads were surprisingly passable; but the
organization, though thoroughly planned, proved less than perfect
in action. Those on the hill passed along the prairie, the two roads
uniting at some distance ahead. This, said Brigham, "caused some
derangement of the already imperfect organization." Members of
the same company were separated, and in trying to get together,

wagons ran into one another and several were damaged. As a result, despite some of the best traveling weather they had encountered, they had moved but ten more miles, twenty-three miles from Nauvoo, and nearly a month had passed since the first teams had crossed the Mississippi.

The next morning, Brigham called on a group of men to move forward as pioneers, cutting and trimming trees and repairing the bad places in the road; they were the guard to carry axes instead of guns and to help every team that was in need of help. "Men must not crowd upon each other, ox teams must give the road and let horse teams pass. When we get properly organized, no two teams must come within two or more rods of each other."[8]

Brigham led his Camp of Israel another nine miles or so, camping near the little town of Farmington, on the Des Moines River. Then came an important turn in their fortunes. William Clayton told the story when he wrote:

> A number of citizens from Farmington came to the camp and gave a very pressing invitation for the band to go to Farmington and play some. Accordingly, about three o'clock, the band started and arrived at Farmington about 4:30 P.M. We played at the principal hotel and then went to the school house and played until nearly dark. The house was filled with men and women, the leading people of the place. We then returned to the hotel, where they had provided us with a good supper. Kay sang a number of songs. By eight o'clock we returned and when we left they gave us three cheers. When we arrived at the camp, we met thirty of the guard just starting out to meet us. The President felt uneasy at our staying so long, and was sending men to protect us.[9]

Invigorated by their experience of the night before, the band started out the next morning without feeding their teams. This required an unplanned stop during the day. The camp crossed the Des Moines River at Bonaparte, negotiated some damp soil, but still had their best day's travel on the trip, sixteen miles, bringing them almost fifty miles from Nauvoo.

The band's reputation, meanwhile, was spreading. The town of Keosaugus, a few miles farther west, invited them to play on three consecutive days. William Clayton reported that they were showered with meals, groceries, and other gifts, and received more than fifty dollars in cash, a welcome fund to buy more food along the way.

These exiles were a gifted group, not only musicians, but poets such as Eliza R. Snow, Parley P. Pratt, and John Taylor; scholars such as Orson Pratt, who was a philosopher, astronomer, and mathematician. The culture to which they were accustomed was now being buffeted by the hazards of western travel.

Often there was sickness in the camp; there were deaths and there were births. Eliza R. Snow and John R. Young, in memoirs written years later, both told of nine babies being born in the first night of the Sugar Creek encampment. Trying to confirm this from more contemporary records, such as those of Brigham Young, William Clayton, or Hosea Stout is fruitless. We must conclude that the figure is a composite one, or refers to other occasions.

Probably the most active midwife in the camp was Patty Sessions. She was possibly as experienced a pioneer as anyone in the camp. She and her husband, David, and their family had accepted the message of the restored Church at their home in Maine in 1834. In 1837, they left for Kirtland, Ohio, where they hoped to join the first main body of the Church. They arrived just in time to join the major exodus of the Church from Kirtland to Far West, Missouri, and endured the final persecutions that drove the Saints into Illinois. In less than seven years, they were on the trail again, exiles from Nauvoo on their way to a new Zion somewhere in the West.

Patty had celebrated her fifty-first birthday on February 4, 1846, the day the first wagons crossed the Mississippi for the encampment on Sugar Creek. Within a few days, she and David were in that shivering and miserable encampment; and before the camp broke and began moving westward, she was exercising her skills as a midwife. Her diary and account book have survived, and it reveals much about the conditions and trials of the long, weary march across Iowa.[10]

The first entry in her account book reads "DR to Patty Sessions for attendance, February 25, 1846, Jackson Redding, $2.00 paid." This would probably have been Return Jackson Redden, known to have been among the earliest Saints to leave Nauvoo. The names of the mothers are seldom listed.

On February 28, Patty attended the wife of John Scott and was paid $2.00, apparently the standard fee. These two births are the only ones listed during the encampment at Sugar Creek.

As the camp moved on, the births continued. There is an illegible entry on March 2, for $2.00, and on March 3, there is a charge to Ezra Benson for $2.00, apparently paid in installments: $1.00,

75 cents, and 25 cents. Ezra gives his own account of this birth in an autobiography provided for Brigham Young some months later:

> After the cold weather abated a little, the different camps took up their line of march through the rain, sleet and mud; the nights were very cold and frosty. My wife Pamelia gave birth to a daughter, about eleven o'clock on the 9th of March. It rained hard. We had nothing but a tent to cover her and had to raise her bed on brush to keep her from the water. Here the camps remained for several days in consequence of incessant rains, which softened the land and made it difficult to travel, as the wheels of our wagons would sink at times to the hub. We named our child Isabella.
>
> The roads being so bad, I went to Brother Brigham and told him I could not proceed any further on account of the heaviness of my load and the weakness of my team. I told him I was willing to tarry there until I could get on further, to which he replied that I must not stop but go on with him and the camp; he asked what I had for loading. I replied, "six hundred pounds of flour and a few bushels of wheat, etc." He said, "bring your flour and meal to my camp and I will lighten you up." I accordingly complied, and to my surprise he requested John D. Lee to weigh it out and divide it among the camps, leaving me about fifty pounds of flour and a half bushel of meal to support myself and family going into a wilderness country.
>
> When we started, I found my wagons rolled comfortably along, while many of the companies' wagons would sink to their axles in the mud, and I would say to them, "go to Brother Brigham, and he will lighten your loads."[11]

Ezra Benson appears again in Patty Sessions's account book on May 1, for he had another pregnant wife. She was Pamelia's sister, Adeline. Adeline's call for assistance from Patty Sessions came at a trying time in Patty's journey. In her diary and account book, she recalled:

> Wednesday, April 29th. . . . rain, and it is very muddy. I lay here in the wagon, my bed and pillows wet, and I cannot set up but a few minutes at a time. 2 o'clock, Brother Brigham came and laid hands on me. I felt better, but could not set up. 7 o'clock at night, Brother Benson came after me. Alline was sick. I got up but could hardly stir. He took me out of the wagon and helped me to his tent. I could not set up, but went to bed, as my labor was not needed at the present.
>
> Thursday, 30th. I came home. Could hardly reach the wagon, went to bed, rested some. About noon I thought I could eat some peach pie. I had a kettle of coals on the wagon. I cooked the peaches on them, and by laying down and resting several times, I made me a pie, went to the stove and baked it. Have eated some and feel better. Sister Rockwood made me some porridge yesterday and some barley coffee today.
>
> Friday, May 1st. Brother Benson came over last night again. I went, found Alline sick. I came home, got some medicine, went back and stayed all night. At nine o'clock a.m. she had a son, William.

Benson family records show that the baby born on May 1 was George Taft Benson, grandfather of President Ezra Taft Benson, President of The Church of Jesus Christ of Latter-day Saints. Patty's account book shows a charge to the first Ezra Taft Benson of $1.50 for services rendered.

Patty Sessions' services to the Saints can hardly be overemphasized. Burdened with problems of her own, she tried to ease them through a life of service to others. Her diary and account book show numerous visits to those sick and distressed for which she received no pay, and the $1.50 and $2.00 entries show she delivered nineteen babies before the Saints were settled in Winter Quarters. The list includes children of such Church leaders as Parley P. Pratt, Hosea Stout, and Amasa M. Lyman. It also includes a mother listed only as "Black Jane." She and her husband lived with a Brother Dikes. The account book shows she charged "Black Jane" one dollar for her services, and the diary shows Brother Dikes paid her with 24 pounds of flour, which he valued at 4 cents a pound, but, she noted, "others asked 2." Her diary is filled with accounts such as these:

> Monday, April 6th. The Church is 16 years old today. It rains hard. . . . Had to double-team all the way through mud and rain, eat on our way, while the team goes back after Brother Rockwood's wagon. Here we camped. . . . We got supper and went to bed and it soon began to thunder and lighten, and rain came faster than ever.
>
> About four o'clock in the morning, I was called on to go back two miles. It then snowed. I rode behind the man through mud and water, some of the way belly deep to the horse. I found the sister I was called to in an old log cabin. Her child was born before I got there. She had rode 13 miles after she was in travail, crossed the creek on a log after dark. . . .
>
> Tuesday, April 7th. The ground froze some. I got on to the horse on a man's saddle, rode home to our wagon. The man went on foot with me. I got home safe.

And then Patty wrote:

> Monday, May 25. Rains this morning again. Brother Kimball came to the wagon, said I must not feel bad. I was crying when he came. I could hardly tell him for what, for I had many things to hurt my feelings. I told him some things. He said everything would be all right, and not to give way to my feelings.

Later in the diary, the causes of Patty's grief began to appear evident. She was fifty-one years old; her husband, David, was fifty-six. In their travels around the country, from Maine to Kirtland, to Missouri, and to Nauvoo, they had buried five of their eight children. Surviving were their eldest, thirty-two-year-old Peregrine, who had a family; twenty-eight-year-old Sylvia, married to Windsor P. Lyon; and twenty-four-year-old David.[12] She hoped and prayed that all of her children might be with her to travel across the plains together. Then she had learned that both Sylvia and young David would wait until next year. But Peregrine was on his way, and was bringing Rosilla with him.

Comparatively late in life, Patty's husband had decided to observe the principle of plural marriage and had taken to wife a much younger woman than Patty; her name was Rosilla Cowen. In accordance with Church policy he had done so with Patty's consent. There is every indication that she welcomed Rosilla when she arrived with Peregrine and his family on June 22, 1846. But there were troubles ahead.

Her diary on June 2 begins: "I slept alone." A week later she wrote: "I have slept but little. I feel as though my heart would break." And the next day: "Sorrow of heart has made me sick. I lay in the wagon all the forenoon. Have many more hard things said to me, but the Lord supports me." On July 11 Patty recorded: "I eat my breakfast, but I am so full of grief there is no room for food, and I threw it up." On the next day: "I feel some better. He has promised to treat me well."

There are many such notations of Patty's grief, which certainly contributed to her breakdown and to her coming near death. But, with her recovery, the troubles with Rosilla continued. David's second wife refused to do her share of the work. She was insulting in her speech. On September 24, the day when the Camp of Israel began to move from Cutler's Park into Winter Quarters, Patty's journal reads: "Rosilla came back. I went and tried to talk with her, but she was very abusive to me until P. G. (Peregrine) told her to hold her tongue, or he would roll the wagon away with her in it."

Following church services on Sunday, Patty decided it was time for a showdown with the younger wife. She recorded:

> Went to meeting; then Mr. S. and I had a talk with Rosilla. She was very wilful and obstinate. He told her to come into the tent, and if she did right she would be used well. I told her it was a big cud for me to swallow, to let her come in after she had abused me so shamefully. . . .

He knew he had done wrong and abused me bad and he was sorry
and shamed of it, and if I would forgive her and let her come in, he
would not do it any more, and would sleep with me when I was at
home, and use me well, and he knew she had abused me worse than I
had her. I said if she came in, I should be boss over the work, and she
must be careful how she wilted and flury at me, without more humility
in her than I could see then, I could bear but little from her. We left
her and went home to bed.

There were other disputes. David tried to solve the problem
by finding employment for Rosilla with another woman, but
Rosilla refused. Finally, according to Patty, "he hauled Rosilla's
things to the river and left her there." Still anxious to do his duty
by his second wife, David crossed the river several times to help
Rosilla, but on December 3, Patty wrote: "Rosilla started for
Nauvoo."

Patty was again busy with her midwifery. She was safely
housed in Winter Quarters, and her account book shows thirty-nine
babies delivered there during the winter of 1846-47. All the trials
of Iowa were behind her. At Winter Quarters she was happy and
ready to travel toward another Zion as soon as the Lord commanded.

The trials of Patty Sessions were duplicated or surpassed many
times by the thousands who finally found Winter Quarters a sur-
cease from their labors. William Clayton, author of "Come, Come,
Ye Saints," had experienced tribulation, and yet he wrote the words
"Come, come, ye Saints, no toil nor labor fear" and "Why should
we mourn or think our lot is hard? 'Tis not so; all is right." On
April 15, he received word from Nauvoo that his wife Diantha had
safely delivered a baby boy. The feeling that all was well swelled
within him and burst forth into song.[13]

There were times when the words "why should we mourn?"
or "all is well" might stick in the throats of the Saints. Even for
Brigham Young, there were many occasions when his lot was hard.
April 6 was the sixteenth anniversary of the organization of the
Church, and the events of those sixteen years rolled through his
mind in a torrent: the years of triumph and tragedy at Kirtland,
the glorious dedication and the grim forsaking of the temple, the
journey to Missouri, the promised Zion of his beloved leader,
Joseph Smith. There followed the wearisome exodus to Illinois,
some happier years in the building up of Nauvoo and the prospering

of the Church in Great Britain, and then the supreme tragedy: the martyrdom of Joseph and Hyrum.

On this sixth day of April, celebrations of the Church's anniversary were held in Nauvoo, where there were still enough Saints left to hold a three-day conference, and in England, where more and more converts were preparing for their journey to Zion. As for Brigham Young, he had not time to give the day more than passing attention. It rained all day, but the wagons started moving at 6 A.M., double-teaming to traverse the water and mud. Brigham wrote:

> We herded our teams as there was no corn in camp. It thundered and lightninged at intervals all day, with a strong northwesterly wind which prostrated a tree, twelve inches in diameter, across Brother Tanner's wagon, in which were three persons, who escaped unhurt. . . . The tents of the second and fourth companies were mostly blown down. I was in the rain all day, arranging the wagons, pitching tents, chopping wood until all were comfortable. Dr. Richards' tent pins were sometimes flying through the air; Dr. working in his shirt sleeves until he was wet to the skin, sometimes lying flat on the ground, holding down the tent while the pins were being driven.
>
> On that day, the Camp of Israel traveled three miles.[14]

This sixth day of April should have been the day for the dedication of the Nauvoo Temple. It was exactly five years earlier when, with great ceremony, four cornerstones for the edifice were laid, and the work began.[15] Brigham Young, with nearly all the Quorum of the Twelve, were in England at the time, helping the newly formed British Mission to prosper; but he returned to Nauvoo and saw the overwhelming sacrifice by the Saints to complete their temple, even when they had learned they must soon leave it. When the final capstone was set in place, Brigham led the Quorum of the Twelve and the congregation in a glorious "Hosanna Shout," thrice repeated. This was not a dedication, but ordinance work was authorized and proceeded at a frantic pace as Saints sought to finish their endowment work before heading into an unknown wilderness.[16] Now, with another April 6 on the calendar, the temple was still not dedicated.

On April 26, Shadrach Roundy arrived in camp. Riding horseback as a messenger, he was but three and a half days out of Nauvoo and carried with him twenty-eight letters. One of them, addressed to Elder Young, was from Elder Orson Hyde, of the Quorum of the Twelve, informing Brigham Young that a wealthy Catholic bachelor wanted to buy the temple and thereby immortalize his name. Orson believed the man would pay two hundred thousand dollars for the property. Brigham presented the matter to his council and there was much discussion. To Bishop Newel K. Whitney, it just didn't seem right to sell the temple. He finally relented, and the word went back that it should be sold.

Apparently the deal was never consummated, and before Shadrach Roundy was back in Nauvoo with the word, the soon to be abandoned temple had been dedicated—twice. On the night of April 30, two members of the Twelve, Orson Hyde and Wilford Woodruff, presided over a dedicatory session at which only select officials were present. The dedicatory prayer was by Brigham's brother Joseph Young. The following day, there was a public dedication with the dedicatory prayer by Elder Orson Hyde, the senior member of the Twelve. An admission charge of one dollar was collected for this dedication, the funds to be used for paying the hands employed on the temple.[17]

The arrival of Wilford Woodruff in Nauvoo, fresh from supervision over the Church in Great Britain, emphasized another problem of the westward migration. Elder Woodruff arrived April 13, completing the second of his major missions to Britain, where his work ranked him among the greatest of missionaries. On December 21, 1840, he had written in his journal, "It is with no ordinary feelings that I meditate upon the cheering fact that a thousand souls have been baptized into the new and everlasting covenant in about half a year, in one field which God has enabled to open."[18]

With leadership and missionary zeal from the entire Quorum of the Twelve, the work in Britain continued to prosper. In the years 1841 through 1845, thirty-three sailing vessels, chartered by the Church, sailed for the New World, carrying 4,503 converts to the restored Church. Nearly all of them sailed from Liverpool, spent weeks and sometimes months on the sea, and then traveled up the Mississippi by riverboat to Nauvoo.[19] In 1846, hundreds of them were numbered among the throngs fighting through the mud and rain and snow of Iowa.

Brigham contemplated many times the importance of this continuing flow as he confronted the problems of his own personal travel; the arrival of Wilford Woodruff could only increase the consciousness that the immigration must continue with minimum interruption. The converts would come from many other places besides the British Isles. By 1846, full-time missions were flourishing in the eastern states and halfway across the Pacific in the Society (Hawaiian) Islands, while individual missionaries had touched upon even more remote corners of the world. The work would go on, and the flood of converts would continue. Hurrying across Iowa to catch Brigham Young, Wilford Woodruff passed company after company of struggling Saints and described one scene when he wrote: "I stopped my carriage on the top of a hill in the midst of a rolling prairie where I had an extended view of all about me. I beheld the Saints coming in all directions, from hills and dales, groves and prairies, with their wagons, flocks and herds, by the thousands. It looked like the movement of a nation."[20]

On April 24, Brigham Young may have been thinking about "the movement of a nation" when the pioneer company crossed the Weldon Fork of the Grand River and reached a delightful site that they soon named Garden Grove. Grass was deep for the grazing of their animals, wild onions flourished in great abundance. There were many wild strawberries, a special delight to Heber C. Kimball. He wrote in his journal: "Here I am with thirty in my family, and not one mouth full of meal, nor have had for two weeks. . . . I am brought to this with hundreds of others on account of so many coming on this journey without provisions to last them a week."[21]

Sixty-nine days had elapsed since the departure from Nauvoo, and the Saints had traveled but 155 miles, an average of about 2½ miles a day. Brigham thought of the thousands on the road and of the thousands more waiting for the opportunity to travel to Zion. The site of Garden Grove looked more and more entrancing, and Brigham made one of the more important decisions of the journey.

The Saints went to work and in three weeks they had broken 715 acres of Iowa sod and had begun planting crops. Homes were built, streets were laid out, and a post office was established. Seeds had been among the important items the pioneers had been urged to bring with them, and soon there were plantings of corn, beans, peas, buckwheat, potatoes, pumpkins, and squash.

On Sunday, the camp assembled for a formal meeting and Brigham explained the reason for the Garden Grove settlement. He said:

> He that falters or makes a misstep can never regain that which he loses. Some have started with us, have turned back, and perhaps more will, but I hope better things of you, my brethren. We have set out to

find a land and a resting place, where we can serve the Lord in peace. We will leave some here because they cannot go farther at present. They can stay here for a season and recruit, and by and by pack up and come on, while we go a little farther and lengthen out the cords and build a few more Stakes, and continue on until we gather all the saints and plant them in a place where we can build the House of the Lord in the tops of the mountains.[22]

Samuel Bent was chosen to preside over the Saints at Garden Grove, with Daniel Fullmer and Aaron Johnson as his counselors. Samuel Bent, a valiant worker in the Church since its Kirtland period, died in service at Garden Grove on August 16, but a successor was soon chosen and the work went forward.[23]

It was May 12 when Brigham Young and his company left Garden Grove. Any realistic hope of reaching the mountains that year must have vanished already, but Brigham continued to talk about it. After four days in Garden Grove, it rained all day, and Brigham Young was not well. It rained all night and all the next day, but at the sound of the horn, the brethren assembled. Parley P. Pratt told them they had been called together to outfit a company of one hundred young men "to go over the mountains and put in crops."

As the rain continued, it was not difficult to convince the Saints at Garden Grove that only a select one hundred young men should go to the mountains that year. Brigham estimated that each person would require twenty-five pounds of flour, and some salt. He felt that one wagon with four oxen and mules and one cow would be required for each four persons. The meeting unanimously approved the Council's decision. Summer was coming on and would be all too short, and winter would find them encamped somewhere, but not in the valleys of the mountains.

On May 18, the main body of the Saints arrived at a place called Mount Pisgah. Only a cemetery remains of the Mormon city that stood there from 1846 to 1852. From that site, the traveler can look westward over rolling plains and hills that seem to go on forever, and perhaps share the feelings of Parley P. Pratt when he named the place. He had been sent ahead to scout out the best location for another semipermanent encampment. He knew when he had found the place, as he later wrote:

> I came suddenly to some round and sloping hills, grassy and crowned with beautiful groves of timber; while alternate open groves and forests seemed blended in all the beauty and harmony of an English

park. . . . As I approached this lovely scenery, several deer and wolves, being startled at the sight of me, abandoned the place and bounded away. . . . Being pleased and excited at the varied beauty before me. I cried out, "this is Mount Pisgah!"[24]

President Young and the rest of the company liked the name, and they liked the place. The plows were soon at work and several thousand acres of rich bottom land along the middle fork of the Grand River were ready for planting. As at Garden Grove, a Church organization was established with a presiding elder and two counselors. Like Samuel Bent at Garden Grove, Presiding Elder William Huntington died in service at Mount Pisgah.

The pattern of the migration was now clear. To provide for the many thousands yet to come along the trail, crops would be harvested; facilities for building and repairing wagons would be ready. Later, both Garden Grove and Mount Pisgah would supply grain and vegetables to strengthen the inadequate diet of the Saints at Winter Quarters.

But in May of 1846, there was still talk of going to the mountains that same year. On Sunday, May 24, it had rained all morning and at noon the horn sounded for the Saints to assemble. Brigham recorded, "Only a few came out. . . . I addressed them the time had come when I should command them what to do, inasmuch as they were not willing to listen to counsel."[25]

His First Counselor, Heber C. Kimball, was even more emphatic. He told his listeners that if they did not improve, the Twelve would go into foreign countries and raise up a body of people who would be willing to abide by counsel and act as becomes the Saints of God.[26]

Both Brigham and Heber, tired and overwhelmed by problems, were obviously becoming testy. It was June 3 when members of the Quorum and a large number of followers left Mount Pisgah, leaving perhaps half of the company to cultivate fields and build houses. Four days into the journey toward Council Bluffs on the Missouri, the company paused to observe the Sabbath. A circle was drawn in front of the tents, a stand erected, and the company was called to services. In his sermon, Brigham Young finally admitted, "I can safely prophesy that we will not cross the mountains this season, and that is what many of the brethren wish; they would rather go to hell than be left behind."

Within a few days, the question of going on to the mountains

in 1846 was decided by another event. On June 26, Captain James
Allen of the United States Army arrived in Mount Pisgah, accompanied by two dragoons. He carried a circular, which he presented
to Apostle Wilford Woodruff and to William Huntington. The circular read:

> I have come among you, instructed by Colonel S. W. Kearny of
> the U. S. Army, now commanding the army of the west, to visit the
> Mormon camp, and to accept the services of four or five companies of
> the Mormon men who may be willing to serve their country for that
> period in our present war with Mexico; this force to unite with the
> army of the west at Santa Fe and be marched thence to California,
> where they will be discharged. . . .
>
> This is offered to the Mormon people now. This year, an opportu-
> nity of sending a portion of their young and intelligent men to the
> ultimate destination of their whole people, and entirely at the expense
> of the United States, and this advanced party can thus pave the way,
> and look out the land for their brethren to come after them.
>
> The pay of a private volunteer is seven dollars per month, and the
> allowance for clothing is the cost price of clothing of a regular soldier.[27]

Captain Allen was directed to Council Bluffs, where he caught
up with Brigham Young and repeated the offer in more formal
language. This was the inception of the Mormon Battalion. It would
provide the solid reason Brigham Young needed for failure to march
to the mountains in 1846. Reason told him, much earlier, that the
trek would be impossible that year. Now, he could point out that
five hundred of their youngest and finest had already gone westward. On August 4, he wrote in his journal, "went up the river to
find winter quarters."

Chapter Four

FIVE HUNDRED GOOD MEN

Brigham Young knew it would not be easy to enlist the five hundred men, who would become known as the Mormon Battalion. From Council Bluffs he hurried back to Mount Pisgah, where he was able to convince sixty-six men to volunteer. There, on July 7, he wrote a letter to President Samuel Bent and his Council at Garden Grove. After explaining the call for men to assist in the war against Mexico, he wrote: "The thing is from above, for our good, has long been understood between us and the U. S. Government."[1]

There were many among the Saints who saw the source of the request to be more earthy. As Zera Pulsipher, one of the first Seven Presidents of the Seventies saw it: "Five hundred of our young men were demanded by the general government through the influence of old Tom Benton, who was a noted mobber in the first Missouri persecutions, and was then in the Senate. This left the Church with old men, children and many poor women, while their husbands were fighting the battles of the United States."[2]

Sergeant Daniel Tyler, who joined the battalion in response to Brigham Young's appeal at Mount Pisgah, explained years later the feelings of many of the Saints:

> It may well be imagined that many of the Saints hesitated about responding to this call. It was not from lack of courage either. The danger of such an expedition would never have caused them to shrink or falter; but they had been deceived so many times by those who held authority in the nation that they looked upon this new requisition with distrust.
>
> The Saints were in peculiar circumstances. They were scattered all the way from Nauvoo to Council Bluffs, and even west of there, for some had crossed the Missouri. They were destitute, having been forced to part with nearly every available thing to procure breadstuffs. The poor and sick and helpless who had been left in Nauvoo were looking

to those in advance camps to help them, and many of the latter were
under promise to do so. Responding to the call would prevent the pioneer
company, which for several days previously had been making preparations to start, from pushing forward to the mountains that year. How
would the helpless women and children do if the fathers and brothers,
upon whom they had depended for support and protection, were taken
away? These were questions that were bound to arise.[3]

Zera Pulsipher's condemnation of Missouri Senator Thomas
Hart Benton may not have been entirely groundless. Zera had led
a caravan of sixty-five wagons in the exodus from Kirtland and
had experienced some of the worst of the Missouri mob actions
that drove the Saints into Illinois. He was probably well acquainted
with the part Thomas Hart Benton had played in the mob and
would not hesitate to blame him for the call of the Mormon Battalion.[4]

On at least two occasions, in later years, Brigham Young himself blamed Thomas Benton for the battalion call. When he blessed
returning members of the battalion in Salt Lake City, he told them,
"The plan of raising a battalion to march to California, by a call
from the War Department was devised with a view to the total
overthrow of the Kingdom of God and the destruction of every
man, woman and child, and was hatched up by Senator Thomas
H. Benton."[5] Still later, the plot was explained in more detail when
Brigham wrote:

> I knew then as well as I know now that the government would
> call for a battalion of men out of that part of Israel, to test our loyalty
> to the government, Thomas H. Benton, if I have been correctly informed,
> obtained the requisition to call for that battalion, and in case of non-
> compliance with that requisition, to call on the militia of Missouri and
> Iowa, and other states if necessary, and to call volunteers from Illinois,
> from which state we had been driven, to destroy the Camp of Israel.
> This same Mr. Benton said to the President of the United States in the
> presence of some other persons, "Sir, they are a pestilential race and
> ought to become extinct."[6]

If Brigham Young suspected such a plot at the time he received
the call for five hundred volunteers, he made no reference to it.
Instead, he took pains in his journal to outline the history behind
the visit of Captain Allen to the Camp of Israel. On Brigham's
way back to Mount Pisgah to recruit battalion members, he met
Jesse L. Little, who was President of the Church's Eastern States
Mission. Elder Little had arrived to report to the President of the

Twelve on a diplomatic mission that had begun the previous January. Elder Jesse Little's formal report begins by quoting Brigham's commission to him:

"Temple of God, Nauvoo, January 26, 1846. If your government shall offer any facilities for emigrating to the western coast, embrace those facilities if possible. As a wise and faithful man, take every advantage of the times you can. Be thou a saviour and a deliverer of that people, and let virtue, integrity, and truth be your motto—salvation and glory the price for which you contend."

In consonance with my instructions, I felt an anxious desire for the deliverance of the Saints, and resolved upon visiting James K. Polk, President of the United States to lay the situation before him, and ask him, as the Representative of our country, to stretch forth the federal arm in their behalf.

Elder Little prepared for his visit to the president. He obtained a letter of introduction to George Bancroft, Secretary of the Navy, from Governor John H. Steele of New Hampshire, and from "other philanthropic gentlemen to the heads of departments." He also held special conferences of the Church in Peterporo, New Hampshire, Boston, New York, and Philadelphia "to take into consideration the most expedient measures for the removal and emigration of the Saints in the eastern states to California."

At the close of the Philadelphia meeting, Elder Little made the acquaintance of a man whose advice and services to the Saints would be valuable for generations to come. He was Thomas L. Kane, the son of Judge John K. Kane of Philadelphia. After hearing Elder Little's recital of the persecution of the Saints and their present condition, Thomas Kane asked to be introduced to the mission president. Their conversation lasted well into the evening and caused Jesse Little to miss the evening session of the conference.

Elder Little recalled his meeting with Thomas Kane two days later. He wrote: "Colonel T. L. Kane called at my lodgings and informed me that he had concluded to go to California with the Twelve and desired letters of introduction to President Brigham Young." Several more meetings between the two were held in the next few days. Letters of introduction were written to Brigham Young and others. At their final meeting, Jesse Little reported: "He gave me much information in relation to our affairs with California, and of affairs at Washington, proferring at any future time to aid me in getting appropriations. After drinking a glass of superior wine together, we separated. I left my blessing upon him, and he gave me the following:

Honorable George M. Dallas,
Vice President of the United States

Dear Sir:

Permit me to give an introduction to you to Mr. J. C. Little, late of New Hampshire, who is chief, or ruling Elder, of the Mormons, or Latter-day Saints, east of the Mississippi.

This gentleman, besides being very highly valued by the members of his own sect, is, I learn, esteemed honest and sincere in his professions by many of our friends in this city. He visits Washington too, I believe, with no other object than the laudable one of desiring aid of government for his people, who forced by persecution to found a new commonwealth in the Sacramento valley, still retain American hearts, and would not *willingly* sell themselves to the foreigners, or forget the old commonwealth they left behind them. Your faithful servant,

Thomas L. Kane

Elder Little arrived in Washington on May 21, 1846, while Brigham Young was still at Mount Pisgah, attempting to decide who, if anyone, should head for the mountains that year. Jesse Little was introduced to President Polk on the day of his arrival. This was formal and preliminary, and before his next visit, he had written the president a long letter outlining the persecutions of the Saints, defending their character, and asking for assistance as they made their way to a refuge in the West. Perhaps exaggerating their numbers, he painted an impressive picture of one of the major migrations of American history. In part, the letter read:

Our brethren in the west are compelled to go, and we in the eastern country are determined to go and live, and if necessary to suffer and die with them. Our determinations are fixed and cannot be changed. From twelve to fifteen thousand have already left Nauvoo for California, and many others are making ready to go. Some have gone around Cape Horn and I trust before this time have landed at San Francisco bay.

We have about forty thousand in the British Isles and hundreds upon the Sandwich Islands, all determined to gather to this place and thousands will sail this fall. There are yet many thousands scattered throughout the States, besides the great number in and around Nauvoo who are determined to go as soon as possible, but many of them are poor but noble men and women, who are destitute to pay their passage either by sea or land.

The president may well have thought that, with so many thousands of Mormons moving westward, it would be easy to supply a thousand or so to serve their country on the way. Those who feel that the Church had no intention of offering soldiers to the nation might ponder the final paragraph of Elder Little's letter, granting that it was written in an atmosphere of national patriotism occasioned by the Mexican War, already under way. It read:

> Believe me when I say that I have the fullest confidence in you, and we are truly your friends, and if you assist us in this crisis, I hereby pledge my life, my property and all I possess, as the representative of this people, to stand ready at your call; and that the whole body will act as one man in the land to which we are going, and should our territory be invaded, we hold ourselves ready to enter the field of battle, and then like our patriot forefathers, with our guns and swords make the battlefield our grave or gain our liberty.

In a few days, Jesse Little was given a three-hour interview with the president, then two more interviews within the next few days. In the third interview, President Polk informed him that the Saints should be protected in California, and five hundred or a thousand of the Saints should be taken into the service, officered by their own men, and that Jesse Little should have letters from him and from the Secretary of the Navy to the Squadron.[7]

A mystery man in the negotiations was Amos Kendall. He was a man of influence in Washington, particularly with the return to power of the Democratic party under President James K. Polk. He held no cabinet post in the Polk administration, but was clearly a man of influence. An avowed expansionist, he had been a supporter of Henry Clay in Kentucky, and by 1846, he could be ranked with those who claimed that the "manifest destiny" of the United States was to expand from coast to coast.[8]

Amos Kendall first appeared on the scene of Mormon history several months before his contact with Elder Little in Washington. In February 1846, prior to the departure of emigrating Latter-day Saints for California, aboard the sailing ship *Brooklyn*, Brigham Young received a letter from Samuel Brannan, who organized and led the voyage. The letter contained a copy of an agreement entered into between Samuel Brannan and A. G. Benson, of New York, who was acting on behalf of Amos Kendall and others. Amos Kendall's name appears nowhere in the contract, but Samuel Brannan explained that "it was drawn up in Kendall's own hand, but no person must be known by Mr. Benson." President Young was given instruction. It read: "Your letter confirming the contract I have made must be written to me, and on the outside addressed to Mr. A. G. Benson, and all will go well."

The proposed contract that Brigham and his Council were asked to approve contained a subtle warning. It pointed out the earnest desire of the migrating Saints "to reach their future home without that molestation on their pilgrimage which the government of the United States, might, under a misapprehension as to their designs, feel themselves called upon to offer." The contract read in part: "A. G. Benson states that he has it in his power to correct any misrepresentations which may be made to the President of the United States, and prevent any authorized interference with them on their journey." In return for the exercise of this amazing power, A. G. Benson and his associates expected a fair reward. If the Saints reached their destination without molestation by the United States, then half of the land that should be granted them by the United States, or anyone else, should be conveyed to A. G. Benson and his associates.

Brigham Young called the Quorum of the Twelve into immediate session and made short work of the offer. He recorded: "The Council considered the subject and concluded that, as our trust is in God and we looked to him for protection, we would not sign any such unjust and oppressive agreement. This was a plan of political demagogues to rob the Latter-day Saints of millions and compel them to submit to it by threats of federal bayonets."[9]

There is no evidence that Jesse Little knew of this strange proferred contract, so decisively rejected by his leaders, when he went to Washington, but he carried with him a letter to Amos Kendall from A. G. Benson. It asked Mr. Kendall to aid Elder Little during his visit to Washington as far as his engagements would permit. Mr. Kendall was the first person Elder Little attempted to visit when he reached Washington. Elder Little found Mr. Kendall ill, but left the letter of introduction and returned the next day. They discussed the subject of emigration and Amos Kendall thought arrangements could be made to assist the emigration by enlisting one thousand men, and arming, equipping, and establishing them in California to defend the country.

Two days later, May 25, 1846, Jesse Little called on Amos Kendall again. The next day, Mr. Kendall informed the Mormon emissary that his case had been laid before President Polk. On June 3, Mr. Kendall conducted Jesse Little to the White House for his first extensive interview with the president. Two days later, the president had made his offer and Jesse Little accepted.

All this information, including the part played by both Mr. Benson and Mr. Kendall, was contained in the detailed report that Jesse Little conveyed to Brigham Young; but Brigham made no mention in his journal of any dissatisfaction with the actions of the men he had once described as "demagogues."[10]

By early July, Elder Little had joined the Camp of Israel in western Iowa and was lending the president every possible assistance in recruiting the Mormon Battalion, the request was reduced from the one thousand mentioned in Washington to five hundred.

Also present to assist the Mormons in every way possible was Elder Little's recently found friend, Colonel Thomas L. Kane. When Jesse Little left Philadelphia for Washington, Thomas Kane was sick in bed. The colonel gave him much advice, wished him well on his mission, and regretted he could not accompany him. On June 5, Elder Little wrote Thomas Kane from Washington, telling him that if he would get up from his couch, his pains would leave him. Two days later he arrived in Washington, still feeble, and traveling against the advice of his doctor, but he assured Jesse Little he actually felt better than when he left home. He was now on a mission to help the Mormons in every way he could. He visited both the president and the Secretary of War to further the promises already made, and he announced his intention to meet Brigham Young and his migrating Saints at the Missouri and then travel westward to California. It was the beginning of a friendship with the Church that would last all of Colonel Kane's life.

He had barely made his acquaintance with Brigham Young when a general meeting was called in a hurriedly constructed bowery at Council Bluffs. Final plans were made for recruiting the remainder of the five hundred volunteers, and the meeting turned into a farewell for the first companies of the battalion, now ready to begin their march toward Fort Leavenworth, where they would be organized for the march to the Pacific coast. Although still in poor health, Colonel Kane attended the farewell party. Four years later, in his address to the Pennsylvania Historical Society, Colonel Kane gave lasting meaning to that gathering in the bowery. He said:

> With the rest, attended the Elders of Israel within call, including nearly all the chiefs of the high council with their wives and children. They, the gravest and most trouble-worn, seemed the most anxious of

any to be the first to throw off the burden of heavy thoughts. Their leading off the dancing in a great double-cotillion was the signal that bade the festivities commence. To the canto of debonair violins, the cheer of horns, the jingle of sleighbells, and the jovial snoring of the tambourine, they did dance! None of your minuets or other mortuary processions of gentles in etiquette, tight shoes and pinching gloves; but the spirited and scientific displays of our venerated and merry grand-parents, who were not above following the fiddle to the Foxchase Inn or Gardens of Gray's Ferry. . . .

Light hearts, lithe figures and light feet had it their own way from an early hour until after the sun had dipped behind the Omaha Hills. Silence was then called and a well cultivated mezzo soprano voice, belonging to a young lady with a fair face and dark eyes, gave, with quartette accompaniment, a little song, the notes of which I have been unable to obtain. A version of the text, touching all earthly wanderers: "Down by the river's verdant side, low by the solitary tide, will Zion in our memory stand—our lost, our ruined native land."[11]

Brigham Young's *Manuscript History* identifies the young singer as Susan Divine, and the song as "The Maid of Judah." The song is preserved in modern Mormon hymnals under the title "Down by the River's Verdant Side." Its words, written about ancient Israel's captivity, are especially appropriate to the 1846 exiles of the Camp of Israel:

> How shall we tune these lofty strains
> On Babylon's polluted plains,
> When low in ruin on the earth,
> Remains the place that gave us birth?[12]

The dance was but the beginning of the special honors paid to the battalion, already a band of heroes. Wilford Woodruff described the scene on July 16. He wrote:

It was a great day in the Camp of Israel. Four companies of volun-teers were organized and ready for marching. They were brought to-gether and formed in a hollow square by their captains. They were then addressed by several of the Quorum of the Twelve, after which the Battalion began its march in double file over the Redemption Hill, seven miles across the Missouri River bottom to the ferry. The brethren who formed the companies left their families, teams, wagons and cattle by the wayside not expecting to meet them again for one or two years. They left their wives and children to their brethren and to the tender mercies of God before they went. With cheerful hearts, they believed they were doing the will of their Heavenly Father. As I viewed them, I felt as though I was looking upon the first battalion of the army of Israel, engaged in the service of the United States.[13]

Surely there were few in the Camp of Israel who did not realize the magnitude of the sacrifice when the journey toward a new Zion was suddenly robbed of five hundred of its most able men. There would be women to take over the duties once performed by their husbands. There would be sons and daughters suddenly advanced to manhood and womanhood in more strenuous work than they had ever encountered. Only a people devoted to eternal principles and followers of men called of God could have found the call of the Mormon Battalion to be a renewed strength rather than a debilitation of their ranks. And yet, in the perspective of nearly a century and a half, it must be accounted that the call of these five hundred good men was a turning point in the destiny of the Saints.

One early benefit was the money earned by members of the battalion, who were paid a minimum of seven dollars a month for a private soldier during their service in the army. On August 28, 1846, Brigham Young visited John D. Lee in his tent. John quoted the President when he wrote: "I have a very dangerous but responsible mission for you to perform. I want you to follow up the Mormon Battalion and be in Santa Fe when they receive their payment. Can you do it?"

John D. Lee was not one to say no to his leader. Under a spiritual adoption practice then current in the Church, he had become Brigham's adopted son. He was soon on his way to Santa Fe, accompanied by another seasoned frontiersman, Howard Egan. By September 17, they had caught up with the battalion. They followed them all the way to Santa Fe and came back with more than $1,200, which would be used to help sustain their families and prepare for the trek westward the next spring.[14]

A winter quarters on the Missouri was already proven a necessity, but the call of the Mormon Battalion made it a certainty. A community of Saints was dedicated to providing for the families of the battalion members and at the same time was preparing for a well-ordered move to the West in the spring. To make that dedication official and purposeful, Brigham Young appointed eighty-eight bishops, "to take care of the families left by the soldiers." They were directed to keep a correct account of "all moneys and other property received by them and how disposed of, at the risk of being brought before the Council and reproved."[15]

The battalion, as it traveled down the Missouri to Fort Leavenworth and then westward toward the Pacific, cherished the promises and admonitions given by Brigham Young, who recorded his
instructions to the men as follows:

> I instructed the captains to be fathers to their companies, and
> manage their affairs by the power and influence of their priesthood,
> then they would have power to preserve their lives and the lives of
> their companies and escape difficulties. I told them I would not be
> afraid to pledge my right hand that every man would return alive, if
> they will perform their duties faithfully without murmuring and go in
> the name of the Lord, be humble and pray every morning and evening
> in their tents. A private soldier is as honorable as an officer if he behaves
> as well. No one is distinguished as being better flesh and blood than
> another. Honor the calling of every man in his place. All the officers
> but three have been in the temple. Let no man be without his undergar-
> ment and always wear a coat or vest; keep neat and clean, teach chastity,
> gentility and civility; swearing must not be admitted. Insult no man.
> Have no contentious conversation with the Missourians, Mexicans or
> any class of people; do not preach, only where people desire to hear,
> and then be wise men. Impose not your principles on any people. Take
> your Bibles and Books of Mormon. Burn up cards if you have any.
>
> Let the officers regulate all the dances. If you come home and can
> say the Captains have managed all the dancing, etc., it will be all right;
> to dance with the world cannot be admitted. . . . Never trespass upon
> the rights of others; when the Father has proved that a man will be his
> friend under all circumstances, He will give to that man abundantly
> and withhold no good thing from him. Should the battalion engage with
> the enemy and be successful, treat prisoners with the greatest civility,
> and never take life if it can be avoided.[16]

The instructions were largely followed, and the promises were
gloriously kept. The only battle the battalion engaged in was with
a herd of wild bulls in Arizona. They completed their mission with
high honors, while their families and fellow Saints undertook the
task of building a city for their winter quarters.

Chapter Five

BUILDING A CITY

Mormon Battalion members who had left their wives and children on the east banks of the Missouri had every reason to believe that they would remain there, in Iowa, near the present site of Council Bluffs. While the battalion was still preparing for its long March, on July 21, 1846, Brigham Young issued a proclamation:

> We would instruct the High Council attend as speedily as convenient to locating and advising all those Saints who will tarry here, as well as others who may arrive this season and locate them here for the winter, or at either of the farms back as circumstances and your best judgment may dictate. . . .
>
> It will not be wisdom for any families to cross the river this season, unless they will have sufficient time to go to Grand Island and cut plenty of hay to winter their cattle and keep them from starving. . . .
>
> It will be wisdom and necessary to establish schools for the education of children during the coming winter in this region, and we wish you to see that this is done.
>
> Done in Council, at Council Bluffs, this 21st day of July, 1846.
>
> WILLARD RICHARDS, Clerk   BRIGHAM YOUNG, President.[1]

A few days later, President Young inserted letters in his journal that were from Lt. Colonel James Allen, the officer who had carried the message requesting the Mormons, and from R. B. Mitchell, an Indian agent, and a letter to the President of the United States from Colonel Thomas L. Kane.

James Allen's letter gives permission for the Mormons to reside for a time on the Pottawatomie lands. Indian agent R. B. Mitchell certified that such action was for the apparent good of both parties. The Pottawatomie Indians were all located east of the Missouri, and their lands would soon become a part of the new state of Iowa. Colonel Kane, whose residence among the Mormons seems to have increased his admiration for them, wrote a forceful letter to the

President, approving the actions of both James Allen and R. B. Mitchell. He nevertheless felt the necessity of warning the Saints to proceed no farther westward.

How then do we account for the fact that, within a week, President Young and most of his Quorum of the Twelve had already crossed the Missouri, with the apparent purpose of making the move permanent? On July 30, Willard Richards, Clerk of the Council, crossed to the east bank "to make out the Nauvoo mail and to close out the unfinished business of the council."[2]

Thus, nine days after the order that it would not be wisdom for any families to cross the river in 1846, Brigham Young and his Council had moved the headquarters of the Church across the Missouri. Perhaps it can best be explained by the westering spirit that pervaded America in that landmark year. Bernard DeVoto appraised in poetic rhapsody the force that was sweeping the nation, including the Latter-day Saints, when he wrote:

> When the body dies, the Book of the Dead relates, the soul is borne along the pathway of the setting sun. Toward that western horizon all heroes of all peoples known to history have always traveled. Beyond it have lain all the Fortunate Isles that literature knows, beyond the Gates of Hercules, beyond the peaks where the sun sinks, the Lapps and the Irish and the Winnebago and all others have known that they would find their happy Hyperboreans – the open country, freedom, the unknown. Westward lies the goal of effort. . . . These people, waiting for spring to come, are enclosed by our myth.[3]

The Mormons, as much as anyone, were caught up in this westward fever. The wide Missouri had been a natural boundary for a generation of westward looking Americans. Brigham Young and his followers could not resist the temptation to cross it, and prepare to go westward with the first breath of spring.

Events that made the move necessary anyhow came somewhat later. They involve the Church's new found friend, Colonel Thomas L. Kane. He was in ill health when he arrived among the Mormons on the east bank. By the time the church leaders crossed the Missouri, his condition had worsened. In mid-August, Brigham Young assisted the colonel to secure a visit from Dr. H. I. W. Edes, an army doctor attached to Fort Leavenworth. The doctor certified, on August 19, that Thomas Kane was suffering from "the violent bilious fever of this region, connecting itself seriously with the nervous system." He prescribed a continuance of the "careful nursing" he was receiving from his friends in the Camp of Israel. Colonel Kane feared he might die among the Mormons and that they might be blamed for his death; he therefore asked a certificate from the doctor as to the excellent treatment he had received.

As his health improved, he had many conferences with President Young concerning the future status of the Mormons encamped on both sides of the Missouri. Colonel Kane's father, Judge J. K. Kane, had called on President Polk to present a plea to permit them to remain on Indian lands until weather permitted travel in the spring. Judge Kane received a favorable reception, but with his report he enclosed a letter of caution from the Office of Indian Affairs. It read:

> A location and continuance for any very considerable length of time near Council Bluffs would interfere with the removal of the Indians, an object of much interest to the people of that part of the country; delay the survey of the lands in question, and thus in all probability bring about a difficulty between Iowa, now about to come into the union as a state, and the general government.

Had Brigham Young had this information earlier, it is hardly likely that he would have advised his followers to remain on the east side of the river. Iowa was no longer Indian territory, and the Pottawatomie chiefs who had signed an agreement to let the Mormons remain on their lands apparently had no authority to make such an agreement. Colonel Kane would soon make this position more clear. By September 7, he was well enough to start on his journey, but before leaving, he asked for a patriarchal blessing from the Church Patriarch, Father John Smith. Normally, patriarchal blessings are given only to members of the Church, but Brigham Young's *Manuscript History* includes the entire text of Father Smith's blessing on the head of "Brother Thomas."

In part it read: "Thy God is well pleased with thine exertions, he hath given his angels charge over thee to guard thee in times of danger, to deliver thee out of all thy troubles and defend thee from all thine enemies. . . . Thy name shall be held in honorable remembrance among the Saints in all generations."[4]

The promises were gloriously kept. While it is believed that Thomas Kane never joined the Mormon church, the Saints never had a better friend. He served in ways that a member of the Church could never have served. His name is revered in the records of the Church, and in the temple, he has, since his death, been given the rites of membership and the endowments of Heaven.

As he left the Camp of Israel to stop at Nauvoo and then proceed to Washington, he carried with him a personal letter from Brigham Young to President James K. Polk. The letter told of a council held with chiefs and braves of the Omaha Indians, and enclosed an agreement signed by Chief Big Elk and others of the Omahas, permitting the Mormons to "tarry on their lands and use what wood and timber would be necessary for [their] convenience while preparing to prosecute [their] journey." The letter mentioned various services the Mormons were planning to render to the Indians: the use of Church teams in harvesting, the storage of corn, building of houses, and cultivating of fields. Similar agreements were reported with the Ponca Indians, a hundred miles to the west, but there was no mention of the Pottawatomies, across the river in Iowa.

The decision to spend the winter on the west side of the Missouri was confirmed, and efforts were under way to locate a satisfactory winter quarters for the Saints. It appeared for a time that this spot might be Cutler's Park, more than a mile west of the Missouri. On Sunday, August 9, Brigham Young wrote in his journal: "Horace S. Eldredge was elected City Marshal for this place, which I proposed to call 'Cutlers Park,' Elder Cutler having first selected the spot."

For the next month, Cutler's Park appears on the date line of most of Brigham's journal entries. Rudiments of city government were established, a brick kiln was planned, a post office was established with Dr. Willard Richards as postmaster. Possibly the first indication of a desire to seek another site came on September 3 when Brigham Young, Ira Eldredge, Jedediah M. Grant, and Heber C. Kimball were appointed by the Council to seek a ferry site, nearly opposite to Cutler's Park. On the same day, Elder Kimball recommended that hay be cut from "the bottom," meaning the Missouri River bottoms. These were among several reasons why it was felt that the Saints should spend the winter nearer to the Missouri. Pea vines along the riverbank would provide excellent grazing. A grist mill might be better established near the mouth of streams that flowed into the river. There was considerable commerce along the river, enabling better connection with the widespread Church. Before mid-September, a search was actively under way for another site. The venerable Alpheus Cutler, for whom Cutler's Park was named, was a member of the committee to locate winter quarters, along with Alanson Eldredge, A. P. Rockwood, J. M. Grant, and Ezra Chase. J. M. Grant was also instructed to visit the Omaha chiefs and invite them to advise with the committee as to the site.[5]

Meanwhile, there were indications that the site should be larger than previously contemplated. On September 9, Orson Hyde reported the names of sixty-four families in St. Louis who were ready to start the westward migration and eighty-two others who would be ready as soon as they could secure the necessary means. In Nauvoo, the forces that would finally drive the remaining Mormons from the city were gathering, and on September 9, twelve teams were ready to leave from Cutler's Park to assist the poor to make the trip across Iowa. The winter quarters about to be established would have to be a place of refuge for more than one winter, perhaps for many.

President Young was interested in gathering the scattered Saints from wherever they were and bringing them to this temporary Zion. Elder Willard Richards read a letter from Joseph Herring, an Indian convert, asking counsel about getting his sister from the Cherokees. It was voted to send a team for her.[6] In the missions of the east and in the British Isles, more and more converts were heeding the call to "come to Zion" wherever Zion might be, and if they came early, winter quarters must be ready for them.

On September 10, the committee on location made its report, recommending a site on both sides of Willow Creek, which entered the Missouri some distance north of Cutler's Park. On Friday the 11th, Brigham wrote: "About half past ten A.M., Elders Heber C. Kimball, Orson Pratt, Willard Richards, Wilford Woodruff, George A. Smith, Amasa Lyman and I walked northwards and located the site for Winter Quarters. After dinner, accompanied by the High Council and Marshall, we returned and I commenced the survey."

He started his task by laying out Main Street, running twenty-two and a half degrees west of north. The other streets were laid off around five acre blocks, each block containing twenty lots.[7] Unnamed at first, the streets were later named for persons important in Mormon history: Smith Street, later named Mormon Street; Joseph, Hyrum, Samuel, and Carlos for the Smith brothers; Cutler, for Alpheus Cutler; and Cahoon, Pratt, Woodruff, Spencer, Hunter, Eldredge, and Chase for others prominent in the migration.[8]

Existing maps of Winter Quarters are unsigned and undated. Thomas Bullock wrote that he drew such a map when he arrived from Nauvoo some two months after the city was first laid out. This may have been the first one.[9] The move into Winter Quarters began on September 23, 1846. Helen Mar Kimball Whitney, who had started her honeymoon with the departure from Nauvoo and had dwelt in wagons and tents ever since, could now look forward to living in a house. Describing the new city, she wrote: "We arrived in our winter quarters about 1 o'clock P.M., which is about 3 miles from Cutler's Park. We are located on the second shelf of the river bottoms. It is laid out in the form of a city, five acres in each block consisting of 20 lots. The city as laid out occupies from six to eight hundred acres of ground."[10]

Her husband, Horace K. Whitney, would begin immediately to build the house that would be their home for the next year and a half. Some of the houses were built hurriedly, and only two days after the move into Winter Quarters had begun, Hosea Stout wrote: "Tonight, myself and family had the pleasure of once more sleeping in our own house for the first time since we left Nauvoo on the 9th day of last February."[11] It was a twelve-by-twelve log structure, as yet without windows or doors, but it was a beginning.

The Whitney house took a little longer. In his journal of November 7, Horace told of roofing and sodding one room, into which they moved that evening. He wrote: "We congratulate ourselves considerably upon being able to live in a house again, as we have got thoroughly tired of living in a tent." His wife added: "We continued to use our wagon as a bedroom until the 30th of November, when it was wanted to bring produce from the country."[12]

A more complete description of this first home of the seventeen-year-old bride was written some years later:

> This, like the majority of the houses was covered with sod, and the chimneys were built of the same. Each room had one door and a window, with four panes of glass, but no floor. I was rather unfortunate, at first, in having a chimney that seldom drew the smoke, particularly when the weather was cold enough to need a roaring fire in front of a good sized backlog, and then being prostrated upon my bed from the 23rd of January until along in March, 1847. It gave me the opportunity of cultivating the qualities of patience and calmness under new vicissitudes from which there was no alternative, only to endure them with as good grace as possible, for many of the Saints were still without a

roof to cover them. But I shed many unbidden tears during the smoking period, lasting one month, when, finding that our fireplace, built of sod, was about to tumble down. The brethren had some bricks brought down from the rubbish of the old fort of Council Bluffs and built a new one. Thus ended our troubles from that quarter.

We had been accustomed to trials from smoke, heat, wind and dust, and many others things of an unpleasant nature, during camp life; and we took considerable pleasure in fixing up our little homes. Our floors we managed to cover with canvas, or pieces of carpeting which had outlived the storm and the wear and tear while journeying from the states. We made curtains serve as partitions to divide the bedrooms, repositories, etc. from the kitchen. Most of our furniture we had made to order, such as cupboards and bedsteads, they being attached to the house; also tables, chairs and stools, and an occasional rocking chair, relics of other days, graced our ingleside. . . . And here I received my "setting out" in crockery ware, etc., which, though not very extensive, was deemed quite immense for those times. Our marriage taking place just as we were about starting from the states, the presenting of these needful articles was postponed till a future time, expecting, as we did then, to cross to the Rocky Mountains before building houses to inhabit. . . .

The larger homes were generally shingled and had puncheon floors with a six lighted window in each room. Father's (Heber C. Kimball) largest house contained four good sized rooms on the ground and two upstairs. My brother William and family lived in one room; my mother, her four little boys, three or four young men and two young women who had been adopted and two of father's wives occupied the rest. The women assisted in sewing and housekeeping.[13]

The Kimball home was probably the largest in the city, and in addition to the house described above, it contained several adjoining row houses, one of them occupied by Helen and her husband. Brigham Young's house was also large, but few details survive to describe it. It was completed on November 12, scarcely six weeks after the move into Winter Quarters. Brigham was a builder by trade, and he evidently built well. Horace Whitney tells of a house warming held on the 12th, with the evening spent in singing and dancing.[14] The next day, a general council meeting was held in Brigham's new home. That evening, a meeting of the Quorum of the Twelve was held there.

Perhaps the most notable of the houses of Winter Quarters was the octagon house of Willard Richards. Dr. Richards was the city's postmaster, and the building was constructed to serve as a home, community gathering place, and a council house. A descrip-

tion of the house, gleaned from Dr. Richards's journals, was compiled by Claire Noall:

> On a snow-whitened day in January, Amelia was petting the chil-
> dren, keeping them as warm as possible in the eight-sided room with
> its small cross-barred windows in two faces, and with a smoke hole at
> the peak of the octagon. A bed occupied each of the six walls for the
> women and children.
> Willard placed his bed along one wall of the extension, next to the
> outside door of the inner room of the wing, one of two compartments.
> In the front room of the wing, he set up a postoffice, with a counter,
> and under a window he arranged a log table for a desk, with chairs for
> his two clerks, Thomas Bullock and Robert Campbell. Boards were set
> up as benches when the council met. Frequently, Willard ate his supper
> with the twelve in his office, his wives waiting upon the men from the
> main room of the octagon. Until the council house could be finished,
> the "Doctor's Tabernacle" served as the community center.[15]

In the exodus from Nauvoo, Dr. Richards's profession as a
doctor of medicine was a sideline at best. He was a Church historian, a faithful secretary to Brigham Young, and especially, he was
a postmaster. He had been given that appointment in March, when
the migration across the Iowa plains finally got under way from
Sugar Creek; and wherever the Camp of Israel halted along the
way, there were packets of mail to be sent and received. Faithful
messengers carried the mail back and forth to and from Nauvoo,
and from there they were sent onward to many parts of the world.

One of the most active of these postal messengers was Orrin
Porter Rockwell. A neighbor of Joseph Smith in upstate New York,
he had been among the earliest to accept the Prophet's message.
He had often served as Joseph's bodyguard, risked his life many
times, and after the Prophet's martyrdom, he continued his devoted
service to the Church. On his mule, with his packet of mail, he
was a familiar sight on the way across Iowa.[16]

Willard Richards as postmaster coordinated all this mail service; and finally, in Winter Quarters, his famous octagon house
played the function of rural post offices across America, a community gathering place. The residence, post office, council house was
made distinctive by its roof, made of straw, mud, thatch, and
willows, slanting upward toward the smoke hole in the roof. Apparently Brigham Young's architectural sense was offended by the
structure. He said it looked like a "New England potatoe heap."[17]

The post office was always a busy place, for Winter Quarters was the head of a worldwide church, and Brigham Young's journal is filled with copies of communications with the heading of Winter Quarters, and addressed to Nauvoo, to England, to St. Louis, and to nearby communities. Winter Quarters was a city born with many suburbs. There was always a community of Saints at Council Bluffs, then often referred to as Council Point. Up the Missouri, 153 miles, Bishop George Miller headed a group of Mormons who had hoped to reach the mountains ahead of anyone else, but had heeded counsel of President Young to wait for springtime.[18] The two Iowa settlements, Garden Grove and Mount Pisgah were continuing their purpose of growing crops and providing accommodations for the thousands yet to come as the great migration would continue through the years.

The post office was but one indication that Winter Quarters was the world headquarters of The Church of Jesus Christ of Latter-day Saints. A busy ferry was in operation on the Missouri by the end of September. John S. Higbee was appointed ferryman, with the privilege of having one or two families locate with him at the ferry. On September 24, Daniel H. Wells and William Cutler crossed on the ferry into Winter Quarters, bringing with them the first news of the Battle of Nauvoo, in which nearly all of the remaining Saints in that settlement were forced to leave—many of them old, some of them sick. Both Daniel Wells and William Cutler had commanded units of the impromptu force that set up cannon and gathered rifles to resist this final attack by mobs. They reported to President Young that a pitiful group of refugees were gathered at Sugar Creek.[19]

Dispatched from Winter Quarters, a rescue group was soon on the way, and by October 9, they had reached the encampment at Sugar Creek. Brigham Young had been especially anxious to give all the aid necessary to the widow of Hyrum Smith. As it happened, Mary Fielding Smith was doing very well. She and her sister, Mercy Thompson, were able to contribute eighteen dollars to assist less fortunate members of the company, and on October 21, the large Smith household arrived in Winter Quarters.[20]

Communications with Saints far beyond Nauvoo was also directed from Winter Quarters. On October 29, Orson Spencer and William Cahoon crossed the Missouri on their way to the British Isles. Orson Spencer bore with him a letter from President Young:

Camp of Israel, Winter Quarters
Oct. 25, 1846

Elder Spencer has been necessarily detained from his mission until the present moment, and as he may not arrive in England until after the departure of Elders Hyde, Pratt, and Taylor, be it known by this letter that Elder Orson Spencer is duly authorized and appointed by our Quorum as above to preside over all the conferences, and Church of Jesus Christ of Latter-day Saints in Europe and her islands, and all the printing and publishing department and emigration of said Church, from the time of his arrival in England.

WILLARD RICHARDS, clerk – Brigham Young
President of the
Quorum of the
Twelve Apostles.[21]

The reasons for Orson Spencer being necessarily detained were well known. On the bitter journey across the Iowa plains, death had claimed Orson's wife, his brother Hyrum, and one of Hyrum's daughters. But Orson Spencer had received the call before leaving Nauvoo to go to England and edit the important Church publication, *The Millennial Star*. Having built a log cabin for his family in Winter Quarters, leaving them to the care of the older children and helpful neighbors, Orson set out to accept his call. His arrival would permit three members of the Quorum of the Twelve, Parley P. Pratt, John Taylor, and Orson Hyde to return to America to care for their families at Winter Quarters and help to prepare the Church for continuing its journey to the West.[22]

Despite the monumental task of supervising the migration of thousands toward their eventual home in the West, the Church leaders felt that the work of carrying the gospel to all the world could not wait. Brigham Young included in his journal a letter from Addison Pratt and B. F. Gronard, writing from the Chain Island, or Ana. This was far south of the Sandwich, or Hawaiian Islands, and near Tahiti. The elders reported ten branches of the Church in that area, and 873 members.[23] For the next year, Church activities of a growing world organization would be reporting to Winter Quarters on the Missouri.

One of the early needs of the settlement was a flour mill. On September 22, the day before the move from Cutler's Park into Winter Quarters began, the Municipal High Council decided to build a mill and appointed Brigham Young as superintendent, with the assurance that Council members would all assist him. Fred

Kesler reported to the group that a mill that would grind one barrel of flour per hour could be built for eight hundred dollars. On the next day, Brigham, with Dr. Willard Richards and Albert P. Rockwood, selected a site on Turkey Creek, not far from the head of Main Street in the early plot of the settlement. By September 29, the Council was ready for bids on the mill. Archibald Gardner contracted to furnish the heavy timbers at $4.75 per hundred, hewn. William Felshaw agreed to do the framing at $1.77½ per square ten feet, and to counter hew. Augustus Stafford would supply the studs, rafters, and braces at $1.35 per hundred, and Ezra Chase would build the dam for $125. By November 1, it was necessary to move the mill site downstream and to recruit men for building a longer mill race.

Completing the mill was a matter of great urgency, and Brigham Young's diary is filled with references to visiting the site. That the completion was eagerly awaited is evident from a year end report where he wrote:

> There had been considerable difficulty to get flour and meal in sufficient quantities to feed the camp; a little grain had been ground at Week's mill (twenty five miles distance, built by the government for the Pottawatomies,) the balance by the mills in Missouri, upwards of 150 miles distant, which made very coarse flour and meal. The inhabitants of Winter Quarters have had to grind wheat and corn by coffee and hand mills, which in many instances only cut the grain, others pounded it with a pestle suspended to a spring pole, and sifted out the finer for bread, the coarse for hominy. Some eat their bread boiled, others boiled their corn in lye to make hominy, while some boiled corn in the ear until it was sufficiently soft to be grated, many pieces of old tin were converted into graters for this purpose. Much anxiety is manifested for the completion of the mill.[24]

In January, work on the mill must have been very limited. On January 6, the thermometer stood at two degrees below zero. This was but the beginning; it was eight below on the seventh, thirteen below on the tenth, and the Missouri River was packed with heavy ice. By the eighteenth, it was a paralyzing twenty degrees below zero. Nevertheless, some work must have continued, for on February 12 Brigham recorded: "I visited the grist mill. Brethren Weeks and Kesler said they ground two to three quarters of corn, one man walking on the wheel and the other feeding the hopper." Evidently there was no water flow to power the mill.

By the time the mill was operating fully by waterpower, Pres-

LDS Historical Church Archives

The mill at Winter Quarters

ident Young was engaged in full-time organization of the pioneer company for the exodus to the Rocky Mountains. But the mill would continue to serve the Saints for another year and would serve others for years afterward. Basic parts of it are included in the structure still standing today. The mill was a source of personal pride to Brigham. Speaking in the Salt Lake Tabernacle eleven years later he said:

> Brethren came to me saying "We must go to Missouri. Can we not take our families and go to Missouri and get work?" Do you know to this day how you lived? I will tell you and then you will remember it. I had not five dollars in money to start with, but I went to work and built a mill, which I knew we would want only for a few months, that cost $3,600. I gave notice that I would employ every man and pay him for his labor. If I had a sixpence I turned it into 25 cents, and a half bushel of potatoes I turned into a half bushel of wheat.[25]

The mill, like many other projects at Winter Quarters, filled a dual purpose: to provide the necessities of life, and to provide employment for suddenly idle hands and minds. By mid-November the sisters were being urged to manufacture willow baskets from the willows that grew in profusion along the riverbank. Members of the Quorums of Seventies were urged to manufacture washboards and tables, and carry them into Missouri to trade for grain and other commodities.

They were also concerned with the building and improving of houses. An excellent source of clay was found and a brickyard was soon established. Nearby, a large supply of rock was found for the "stoning" of wells. The chimneys of Brigham's own house were made with brick hauled from the ruins of an old fort at Council Bluffs. Much of the work was still under way at year's end, and in his year-end report the President described the activity:

> The buildings of the city were generally of logs, averaging from twelve to eighteen feet long, a few of which were split; the floors were laid with puncheon (logs split about three inches thick and hewed on one side.) The timber used for floors was principally lynn and cottonwood; a great many roofs were made by splitting oak timbers into boards called shakes, six inches wide and about three feet long and half an inch thick, which were kept to their places by weight poles, a few were nailed on. Many roofs were made with willows, straw and earth, about a foot thick, while others had puncheon. Many of the cabins had no floors. A few persons who could not procure logs made dugouts on the side hills, cutting out a fireplace at the upper end, the ridge pole of the roof was supported by the uprights in the center. Such were generally roofed with willows, straw and earth. The most of the chimneys were built of prairie sods, and the doors made of shakes pinned together, wooden hinges and finished with a string latch. The log houses were daubed inside with clay; a few rather more aristocratic cabins had fireplaces made of clay pounded in for jams and back. A few persons had stoves.
>
> The building of these houses was prosecuted with unremitting energy; at any hour of the evening the sound of the ax or the saw relieved the stillness of the night.[26]

Thus, under the leadership of a master builder, thousands of men and women, many of them strangers to any kind of pioneer environment, built a city as if building for years to come, not just for one or two winters. They were not only building houses and mills and brickyards, they were building a stalwart community of men and women who were well-equipped for the tasks that were ahead.

Brigham Young was wholly devoted to the Prophet Joseph Smith. In many recorded sermons throughout his life, he quoted the Prophet's words again and again. In trying to govern his people at Winter Quarters, he must have recalled Joseph Smith's story of a man who came to visit him and asked, "How is it that you can control your people so easily? It appears they do nothing but what you say; how is it that you can govern them so easily?" The Prophet answered, "I do not govern them at all. The Lord has revealed certain principles by which we are to live in these latter days. The time is drawing near when the Lord is going to gather his people from among the wicked. . . . The principles which he has revealed I have taught to the people, and they are trying to live according to them, and they control themselves."[27]

At Winter Quarters, Brigham Young found opportunity to apply these principles of self-government in many ways. In a blend of ecclesiastical and democratic government, he brought about the active participation of many able assistants. The Municipal High Council, which was to govern the city, was chosen before the move from Cutler's Park. On August 7, the Camp of Israel seemed so disorganized that Brigham recorded: "I asked the brethren if we should stop here, or look farther, or whether we should settle together or every man for himself. C. P. Lott, Reynolds Cahoon and others spoke in favor of following the counsel of the twelve."[28]

After much discussion, the Municipal High Council was selected, with Alpheus Cutler as President. He was one of the senior citizens of the camp. He had served as a member of the Municipal High Council of Nauvoo and had been a source of wisdom and valiant service to the Saints as they struggled across Iowa. Other members of the Muncipal High Council of Winter Quarters were Reynolds Cahoon, Cornelius P. Lott, Albert P. Rockwood, Ezra Chase, Daniel Russell, Alanson Eldredge, Thomas Grover, Jedediah M. Grant, Samuel Russell, Winslow Farr, and Benjamin L. Clapp.

No member of the Quorum of the Twelve was in the Municipal Council and clearly its functions were subservient to the Twelve. On November 23, the High Council met with the Twelve. President Young explained "to the High Council their duties to attend to temporal as well as spiritual things, and help to bear off the burthens of the Church . . . to take care of the poor and appoint Bishops to do the same, and also to call Bishops to account from time to time and devise ways for the poor to sustain themselves by their own labor instead of calling on the rich to hand out what they have."[29]

It was often hard to separate the temporal from the spiritual. Two of the High Council members, Jedediah M. Grant and Albert

P. Rockwood, were empowered to appoint at least twenty-four police. These were placed under the direction of Hosea Stout as captain. Hosea had been a colonel in the Nauvoo Militia, and when that body was reorganized at Winter Quarters, he was named to a similar position. He had also been a captain of police in Nauvoo.[30] On more than one occasion, it was necessary for Hosea, a strict disciplinarian, to whip miscreants publicly, and such stern actions were approved by Brigham Young.

The office of bishop in The Church of Jesus Christ of Latter-day Saints is always a close combination of the temporal and the spiritual. The bishop is generally considered the father of his ward, a definite geographical entity over which the bishop exercises spiritual and considerable temporal responsibility. The position of bishop took its place in the organizational structure of the Mormons even before the Church was organized; but the early bishops (Edward Partridge, George Miller, Newel K. Whitney) were considered bishops to the entire Church.[31] The word *ward* is not even indexed in the Doctrine and Covenants, and it was not until the Nauvoo period that it was used. It was probably derived from the wards that were districts of the growing city on the Mississippi. Even the diligent researcher B. H. Roberts had difficulty determining the exact number of wards and their corresponding bishops.[32]

At Winter Quarters, there was a transition of the bishop's responsibility to individual geographical wards. On July 17, at Council Bluffs, as the Mormon Battalion was preparing for its departure, the Quorum of the Twelve met and appointed eighty-eight men to act as bishops. This group was called for one purpose only, "to take care of the families that were left by the soldiers." There is little further mention of these eighty-eight bishops and the services they rendered, but by late October, the word *bishop* had begun to take on quite a different meaning. At a High Council meeting on October 25, Brigham Young presented a list of the bishops of thirteen separate wards, each of them comprising one block. They were called upon to report their transactions in their wards, "relieving the poor and the sick, and helping the families in need out of their own pockets." They expressed their determination to attend to their callings faithfully. Brigham asked the bishops to assist him in making sure the families of the brethren in the Mormon Battalion were well cared for and visited. The constant stream of emigrants continued to pour into Winter Quarters, and before the end of the year, the number of wards increased to twenty-two.[33]

Since the Mormon ward has become a vital unit of the Church and the bishop is an indispensable functionary in its operation, the names of these pioneering bishops deserve recording. The first thirteen wards, with their bishops, were as follows:

Levi R. Riter: First Ward
William Fossett: Second Ward
Benjamin Brown: Third and Fourth Wards
John Vance: Fifth and Sixth Wards
Edward Hunter: Seventh Ward
David Fairbanks: Eighth Ward
Daniel Spencer: Ninth Ward
Joseph Matthews: Tenth Ward
Abraham Hoagland: Eleventh Ward
David B. Yearsley: Twelfth Ward
Joseph B. Noble: Thirteenth Ward

Most of these bishops remained in service when the wards were increased to twenty-two, but in some cases were assigned to different wards. As the city grew, many ward boundaries were changed. The following were the new assignments, with the boundaries of the respective wards and the new bishops:

First Ward: All the inhabitants of the south side of Joseph Street, Bishop Edward Hunter
Second Ward: The north side of Joseph Street, David Fairbanks
Third Ward: The south line of Smith Street, Levi Riter
Fourth Ward: Block 24, Daniel Spencer
Fifth Ward: Block 25, Shadrach Roundy
Sixth Ward: Block 26, William Fossett
Seventh Ward: Block 27, Joseph E. Robinson
Eighth Ward: Block 28, Luman H. Calkins
Ninth Ward: Block 29, Dr. Thomas Lang
Tenth Ward: Block 30, Daniel Garn
Eleventh Ward: Block 31, Abraham Hoagland
Twelfth Ward: Block 32, Ephraim Badger
Thirteenth Ward: Block 33, Samuel Rolf
Fourteenth Ward: Block 34, Abraham O. Smoot

Fifteenth Ward: Block 35, Isaac Clark
Sixteenth Ward: Blocks 36 and 41 and north to the creek,
    Benjamin F. Brown
Seventeenth Ward: Block 37, Albert Lutz
Eighteenth Ward: Block 38, John Vance
Nineteenth Ward: Block 39, John Higbee
Twentieth Ward: Block 40 and north to the creek, Joseph B.
    Noble
Twenty-first Ward: All north of the creek and west of Second
    Main Street, Addison Stewart
Twenty-second Ward: All east of Main Street and north of creek,
    Willard Snow[34]

Isaac Clark, bishop of the Fifteenth Ward, left a diary and account book that illustrates how a bishop became the father of his ward. From December 2, 1846, to January 16, 1847, he lists the number of days of work contributed by his members to the building of the mill race and the Council House. On December 7, Norman S. Williamson is credited with four days of work done for George A. Smith for the support of some orphans. On January 1, 1847, the bishop received eighty-one pounds of fish from the fishing company to be distributed among the poor. On March 23, 1847, $10.95 was paid to Asa Lyman for attendance on deceased: $10.50 for services and 45 cents for burial. On May 16, 1847, to Norman Williamson, one pint of whiskey in his sickness, 10 cents. On May 20, another pint through the hands of Jacob Bigler. November 20, distributed to Orson Pratt, one load of hay, $2.25; to George A. Smith, 10 pounds of fish, 22 cents.

The bishop's court, still important in the wards of the Church today, was developed and refined at Winter Quarters. Bishop Clark's records show that on August 11, 1847, a charge was preferred by William Meeks against Harvey Green for unlawfully taking away a part of the fence that protected William's garden. It was decided in bishop's court that the two brethren should shake hands and get together to repair the fence.

No one was above being called into bishop's court. On November 20, 1847, Hosea Stout, the formidable Captain of Police, was hailed into Bishop Clark's court by Hiram Murdock, who accused Hosea of beating him without mercy and without provocation. Bishop Clark proposed that the men arrange the matter like brethren. The police chief refused, saying he had done well and would do it again. The case was tried. Hosea Stout was found guilty, was ordered to pay a three dollar fine, and instructed to acknowledge his guilt before the court. He refused and appealed to the High Council.[35]

In Hosea's own diary, he accuses Bishop Clark of extreme partiality. Brigham Young called the Council and the police together for a meeting. It was decided the case should be dropped to maintain the necessary respect for the police.[36]

The assistance of twenty-two bishops, the Municipal High Council, the Quorum of the Twelve, the police, and others made Brigham Young's task easier and helped him to grow. On the perilous trip across Iowa, he had become testy and sometimes desperate. His conferences with the Quorum of the Twelve, individually and collectively, were frequent and frantic, and he called often for a supporting vote for his position.

It was Winter Quarter, with a chance to appoint and supervise leadership at every level, that turned Brigham Young from a Quorum leader to a confident head of all his people. He instructed his twenty-two bishops to see that there was a school in every ward and to cooperate to build a Council House where all the people could meet together.

Few records have been found of the schools at Winter Quarters, but an interesting account was related years later by Emmeline B. Wells, who at that time was the wife of Bishop Newel K. Whitney. Following his death in Salt Lake City, she married Daniel H. Wells. Recalling the Winter Quarters period, she told the following to Howard R. Driggs:

> Yes, we had our hardships there on the Missouri. There was a great deal of sickness and many deaths, especially of babies and the older folk. Yet, the Lord did not forget us. We had our brighter moments. The brethren built larger log houses in which we could worship and have our social gatherings to sing our troubles away.
>
> I taught one of the schools. You see, I was born and reared in Massachusetts, and was trained for teaching when Horace Mann was a teacher at one of our schools there, and I did teach for two years. Afterward, I joined the Church of Jesus Christ of Latter-day Saints and went west to Nauvoo.
>
> When we left our beautiful city on the Mississippi, I was one of those who got over the Missouri River into the land of the Omaha Indians. Of course I wanted to help, and seeing the number of barefooted boys and girls running about the town, I asked our leaders to build a schoolhouse and let me teach the lively youngsters the best I could.

They were glad to provide the house. It had only a dirt floor, with just logs for seats. We did not have many books and mice ate up some we did manage to gather, but the boys and girls were ready to learn. They recited with me, read what they could, and sang songs. Best of all, they were out of the cold and were kept busy.[37]

In the forge of Winter Quarters, the character of Brigham Young was shaped and supported. Less than four months after the streets were laid off, he prepared a message for all the Saints. He asked for and received the unanimous approval of the Quorum of the Twelve for a revelation he had been given. He presented it to the Saints for their sustaining vote. It was the first revelation announced by Brigham Young, and it bore the title "The Word and Will of the Lord concerning the Camp of Israel in their journeyings to the West."[38]

In the rambling octagon house of Dr. Richards, the revelation was read to each of the governing councils: first to the Municipal High Council, then to the first Seven Presidents of Seventies, and finally to the Quorum of the Twelve Apostles. In each case, the vote was unanimous in support of the revelation. Reynolds Cahoon of the High Council was the first to move that the statement be accepted as the word and will of God. It was then endorsed separately by each member of the High Council. When it was presented to the Seventies, they gave their unanimous endorsement and agreed to do the entire work of laying the floor to the new Council House. After separate approval by the Quorum of the Twelve, the revelation was presented to the entire congregation at a meeting on February 17, 1847. Again, the endorsement was unanimous.[39]

Enthusiastically, Brigham Young had been accepted as a living prophet. It was at Winter Quarters, a place for planning, for organization, and for the application of divine principles that it was all accomplished.

Chapter Six

AND SHOULD WE DIE

It was probably John Ray Young, nephew of Brigham Young, who first described Winter Quarters as "the Valley Forge of Mormondom." He was ten years old when he left Winter Quarters, but he described it years later. He wrote: "Our house was near to the burying ground, and I can recall the small, mournful trains that so often passed our door. I remember how poor and shameful our habitual diet was . . . and the scurvy was making such inroads among us that it looked as if all might be sleeping on the hill before spring."[1]

There are disputes as to how many people actually died at Winter Quarters. A frequently quoted figure is 600, but this would have to include other encampments as well. A careful compilation from contemporary reports shows 302 deaths at Winter Quarters (see appendix). Fifty-seven had died in Cutler's Park; a large number at Council Bluffs, Mount Pisgah, and Garden Grove; and many more were in graves both marked and unmarked on the Iowa plains.[2] There were many deaths such as that recalled by Anson Call. He remembered: "The morning of the 15th of June, 1846, we found Hyrum, our youngest son, dead in his bed. The cause of his death we knew not. He was six months and 12 days old. He was buried at Cedar Creek, near Wesley Cain's sawmill on the south side of the mill, about 50 rods from it by the side of an oak tree. We wrote his name upon the tree."[3]

Other names were hurriedly carved on improvised wooden headboards. Some of the dead were buried in small cemeteries across Iowa, but all were a part of the Winter Quarters experience and are commemorated on the monument standing there today.

There were people such as Theodore Turley, a former Methodist minister, who had joined the Latter-day Saints in Parley

P. Pratt's amazing harvest of souls in Toronto, and who later became one of the first Latter-day Saint missionaries in his native
England. At Winter Quarters, Theodore Turley buried his first
wife, Francis Amelia Kimberley, and her infant son, Jonathan.
Their daughter, Francis Amelia Daniel, wife of Cyrus Daniel, died
during childbirth at Cutler's Park. Theodore Turley had embraced
the doctrine of plural marriage before leaving Nauvoo, marrying
the three Clift sisters: Mary, Eliza, and Sarah Ellen. At Winter
Quarters, he buried Sarah Ellen and three of her children: two-year-
old Princetta and infant twins Joseph Smith and Hyrum Smith
Turley. In all, Theodore Turley buried seven members of his immediate family on the west bank of the Missouri.[4]

Truman Angell, future temple architect, buried a daughter at
Cutler's Park and another daughter and a son at Winter Quarters.
Incredibly, Stillman Pond lost four children, their graves scattered
across the Iowa plains, then four more children and his thirty-four-
year-old wife at Winter Quarters.[5] All of these men remained true
to the faith and became stalwarts in the Church.

A large number of the deaths at Winter Quarters were ascribed
to canker. The first was that of fifty-one-year-old Ashabel Dewey,
October 6, 1846, while the Saints were still moving from Cutler's
Park into Winter Quarters. On November 12, canker claimed the
life of Joseph Woodruff, the infant son of Wilford Woodruff of the
Quorum of the Twelve and his wife Phebe Carter Woodruff. He
was one year old, born in Liverpool, England, before Wilford Woodruff began his journey to join the Saints on their way westward.

On January 31 Wilford, Phebe, and their children set sail from
Liverpool. By the time they reached New York, Brigham Young
and the advance party of Saints were half way across Iowa. The
Woodruffs stopped long enough at Nauvoo for Wilford to attend
two separate dedications of the abandoned Nauvoo Temple, then
hurried across Iowa to join the advance company.

In October, while cutting timber to build houses at Winter
Quarters, Wilford was seriously injured by a falling tree. While
still recuperating, on November 4, he wrote: "Our little boy,
Joseph, was taken sick this day. Had taken cold and it settled in
his lungs. I, this day, for the first time, went out of the wagons,
with the assistance of two persons." But Joseph, the boy whose
birth was greeted with such rejoicing and gratitude in England,
was near death. Wilford wrote:

November 8. I was enabled to walk to the Richards' tent today. Mrs. Woodruff had to spend the whole time day and night, with Joseph, as he is in a dangerous situation.

November 10. Joseph had the appearance of dying in the afternoon and evening, but revived about 12 o'clock.

November 12. Sister Abbott took the main charge of him during the night, as Mrs. Woodruff's strength was mostly exhausted. He had suffered much from convulsions during his sickness, but he breathed his last and fell asleep this morning, 15 minutes before 6 o'clock, and we took his remains to the grave at 4 o'clock this afternoon.

December 8. At half past 3 o'clock this morning, Mrs. Woodruff was delivered of a son, which was untimely, 6 weeks before her time. The boy was alive, smart, and active, and yet we cannot expect him to live but a short time. We call his name Ezra. Mrs. Woodruff is doing as well as can be expected.

December 11. We attended to the burial of our child today, being 2 days old when it died. This is the second son we have buried within a short time. Mrs. Woodruff is quite unwell.[6]

In their travels and trials on behalf of the restored gospel, Wilford and Phebe Woodruff lost four of their nine children.

Little Joseph Woodruff is listed as having died of canker. There were thirty-five others whose deaths were ascribed to that same cause. Most of them were children, but there were others: Ashabel Dewey, 51; Samuel P. Akins, 20; Dolly H. Duncan, 38; Elizabeth Melvil, 25; Margaret Blackhurst, 43; Ann E. Mann, 40; Joanna Roundy, 22; Sally Carter, 21; and Sarah Billington, 27. Canker hit the camp of the Saints first at Garden Grove, where Dr. Willard Richards wrote a description of it: "Here a disease called by the Council of Health black canker began to spread. The patient, stricken with a bilious colic, suffered from chills and fever. A vitiated mucous membrane affected his stomach and bowels. His toes turned black, and as a result of the disturbed circulation, the black stain moved further up the legs. The whole nervous system became involved."[7]

A more vivid description was given by a sufferer who recovered from canker. It is found in the diary of Lovisa Jenne Roundy who married Shadrach's son Jared in 1853. She was but 14 when the family came to Winter Quarters. She recalled:

When we got to Winter Quarters, my Aunt's little girl, 1 year old, died; that left her without a child, and her husband on a mission. That winter, my uncle's plural wife died, and my own dear little brother; then I took sick, was sick all winter, came nearly dying. We had lost at that time four of our dear ones.

The persecutions and hardships we had to go through were unlimited. We had a very poor living, mostly corn meal for bread, no vegetables. It was very hard on the people; caused much sickness. We had what they called scurvy, black leg, and canker; with it I had all three. My mouth was so bad with canker that I never tasted food for six weeks; only as sometimes the folkes would toast some bread, browned it, and made coffee with it and I would drink it. I could only drink, my mouth was so badly eaten with canker, and my legs were all drawn up. I could not straighten them no more than if I was sitting down. They were that way for a long time, but at last they grew some better. Until they were straightened out a little, one of my legs was two inches shorter. I walked with a cane for a long time, but it lengthened to be as long as the other was. I was very thankful for the blessings that God gave us and that we were away from the mob.[8]

Scurvy first appeared on the death list in March of 1847, and claimed twenty-three lives in the next two months. Like canker, scurvy was a vitamin deficiency disease, caused by inadequate diet. In his diary for March 14, Horace K. Whitney described the disease. He wrote: "This disease would start with dark streaks in the ends of the fingers and toes, which increased and spread until their limbs were almost black, causing such intense agony that death would be welcomed as a relief from their suffering. It was caused by want of vegetable food and living so long on salt meat without it.[9]

Horace Whitney was to learn more about scurvy in the weeks to come. His eighteen-year-old wife, Helen Mar Kimball Whitney, suffered with the disease shortly after giving birth to a baby girl who died. Helen wrote:

> Thus, the only bright star to which my doting heart clung was snatched away, and though it seemed a needless bereavement and most cruel in the eyes of all who beheld it, their sympathies were such that by their united faith and prayers, they seemed to buoy me up to that degree that death was shorn of its sting till I could say, "Thy will, not mine be done."
>
> Three weeks of suffering followed; when I was dressed one day, I took cold and was again prostrated and lay in a critical state for another three weeks, a part of that time in a cold, clammy sweat until everything on me was as wet as tho it had been drenched in cold water, and death seemed determined to claim me, but I was saved for a purpose. Before I was able to sit up, the scurvy laid hold of me, commencing at the tips of the fingers of my left hand with black streaks running up the nails, with inflammation and the most intense pain which increased till it reached my shoulder. Poultices of scraped potatoes, the best thing, it was considered, to reduce the inflammation, would turn black as soon as applied, and for all they were changed every few minutes for fresh things, it was all to no effect.
>
> By this time, I had lost all faith and patience, too, and with a

feeling of desperation I arose and, taking my wraps and everything with it, threw it with such force that it went into the fireplace on the opposite side of the room, saying, "There you can stay, for I will never do another thing for it!" To my great surprise, I had no occasion to, as the pain and disease had left me, and from that moment I felt no more of it. Still there were other obstacles in way of my full recovery, though I was free from pain. I remained in a feeble state for some time, so that I had to lie down a goodly portion of the time.[10]

As she recovered, Helen watched one dismal march after another to the growing cemetery on the hill. It had been established by order of the Municipal High Council on November 11, 1846, and several days later the first burial took place there.[11] Within a week there had been six, and by the end of November the new cemetery contained 18 graves. Those who died at Winter Quarters prior to November 16 were buried at Cutler's Park. Among these were Julia Ann Shumway, twenty-eight-year-old wife of Charles Shumway, first of the Saints to cross the river from Nauvoo. She left behind a three-year-old daughter, Harriet, who later died at Winter Quarters, a victim of canker. Harriet was laid in the new cemetery at Winter Quarters. By that time it contained 133 graves. Among them was the grave of Mary Pierce Young, twenty-five-year-old wife of Brigham Young.[12] On March 17, Brigham preached at her funeral, dedicated her grave, and then met with the Captains of Fifties to make final preparation for departure of the company of pioneers.[13]

There were 302 graves on the hill above Winter Quarters when the settlement was abandoned in May of 1848, but there would be one more. On May 21, the steamboat *Mustang* came up the Missouri with a number of Saints from Great Britain. The boat also carried the body of a great missionary, Mephiboseth Sirrine. Elder Sirrine was an early convert to the Church and had already served two missions, one in Michigan and one in the eastern states, when he was called back to Nauvoo and named a Captain of a Hundred when the Saints began their exodus. Before he could begin the journey, however, he was called on another mission, this time to Great Britain. He returned to America in the fall of 1847 and became President protem of branches in the eastern states. In the spring of 1848, he started again for the West, but died of consumption on April 29, 1848, while traveling on the steamboat *Niagara*. He was first buried in Nauvoo, but his family and friends wanted his body to be with the Saints. His remains were exhumed and taken on the *Mustang* to a resting place at Winter Quarters.

His funeral was impressive. President Young, now returned from Salt Lake Valley and named the second President of the Church, was in charge of a memorable service. Apostle Ezra Taft Benson was a member of the procession to the cemetery, as were Elders Erastus Snow and Franklin D. Richards, stalwart members who would soon be called to the Quorum of the Twelve. These leaders escorted Sister Sirrine and her children to the gravesite. It was the 303d burial at Winter Quarters.[14] There would be no more until the old settlement was reborn under a new name; but the old cemetery would remain "Winter Quarters," a sacred name to those who knew and remembered.

Chapter Seven

WE'LL MAKE THE AIR
WITH MUSIC RING

William Clayton's Journal might well serve as a textbook for the ups and downs, the highs and the lows, of Mormon migration. Most of William Clayton's existing portraits make him appear as a man ready to vent his anger against the ills and misfortunes of life. The biography that accompanies his journal agrees with this appraisal. It reads: "As will appear from his portrait on the frontispiece, William Clayton did not tend to frivolity or mirth, but rather to seriousness and earnestness."[1] The journal is filled with accounts of sickness, bad weather, and distress. Yet, within these same pages are accounts of the small but important triumphs that made distress bearable and gave a silver lining to the clouds of sickness and adversity, usually through music.

The fall and winter of 1846-47 were filled with illness for William Clayton. On Tuesday, September 15, he wrote: "This evening I copied a letter to Joseph P. Herring, and having no one to send it by, I took it to council myself. Before I got half way there my knees failed me, and it was with difficulty that I got there and home again." Four days later, he wrote: "Since Tuesday, I have not been out of bed, but today I feel somewhat better again."

Before the end of September, he had managed to join others in the move from Cutler's Park to Winter Quarters, where he started to build two houses for his families. Then, during the month of October, this faithful record keeper failed to make a single entry in his journal. In a simple entry on November 1, he explained that he had been alternately sick and well during the past month, but one house was nearing completion and would soon be occupied. Another month went by without an entry, and still another. When he resumed his diary, beginning with the new year, 1847, William Clayton seemed a new man. He wrote:

Friday, January 1, 1847. Morning at the store. At 2 P.M., went with
Diantha to her father's and partook of a roast turkey for dinner. At 4:00,
met the band at the basket shop and played about an hour and a half.
The basket makers made each of us a present of a new basket and
showed their gratitude various ways. At 6:00, met with the band at
Father Kimball's and played for a party until after one o'clock. Presidents
Young and Kimball danced considerable, and all seemed to feel well.

On January 7 he reported: "Went to Leonard's and played for
them, with Hutchinson and Smithies until 12:00." The next day,
he wrote: "The band met at my house and played some." And on
January 12, he recorded the birth of a son to his wife Ruth: "She
had a hard time, but is comfortable as can be expected. The boy
is named Newel Horace. Evening, I met with the band at Johnson's
and played until 11:00."

William Clayton obviously prized his membership in William
Pitt's band. He had faithfully recorded the triumph as the band
made its way across Iowa, entertaining the countryside and even
making some ready cash to help pay the travel expenses. The band
was present on an important day, that of April 15, 1846. William
Clayton's journal entries for the preceding days had been filled
with gloomy reports on the weather and the mounting difficulties
of travel. A violent windstorm, accompanied by heavy rain, had
blown over all but two of the tents in his company. The ground
had frozen, and then it had rained again. Horses and cows had
broken into some of the tents to find food. Some members of the
band reported they had no meat and no flour. He was worried
about the condition of his pregnant wife, Diantha, whom he had
left in Nauvoo. Then, on April 15, he reported some joyful news:

This morning, Ellen Kimball came to me and wished me much
joy. She said Diantha has a son. I told her I was afraid it was not so,
but she said Brother Pond had received a letter. I went over to Pond's
and he read that she had a fine boy on the 30th ult., but she was very
sick with ague and mumps. Truly I feel to rejoice at this intelligence,
but feel sorry to hear of her sickness. . . .

In the evening, the band played and after we dismissed, the following persons retired in my tent to have a social christening, viz., William
Pitt, Hutchinson, Smithies, Kay, Egan, Duzett, Redding, William
Cahoon, James Clayton and Charles A. Terry and myself. We had a
very pleasant time playing and singing until about twelve o'clock. We
named him William Adrian Benoni Clayton. . . . This morning, I com-
posed a new song, "All is well." I feel to thank my Heavenly Father
for my boy, and pray that he will spare and preserve his life and that
of his mother and so order it that we may soon meet again.[2]

The following evening, Brigham Young promised William that he could send for Diantha and the babe when they reached Grand River. One brief sentence is the only contemporary mention of the birth of "Come, Come, Ye Saints." Soon after it was written, it was made known to the thousands of immigrants who would travel the same route. Its words would sustain them and give them hope beyond the cares of the day. The promises of "we'll find the place which God for us prepared," and "we'll make the air with music ring" would echo around campfires and along the trail for the next twenty-two years, until the railroads made the journey to Zion quite commonplace.

It is probable that the first person to sing "Come, Come, Ye Saints," other than William Clayton himself, was John Kay, the singer in the brass band led by William Pitt. Both William Pitt and John Kay were among those who spent the evening with William Clayton, playing and singing, on the day the song was written. John Kay was a robust man, weighing some 250 pounds, with a rich baritone voice, and equipped with considerable athletic prowess. In his native England, he had soundly thrashed a man who was persecuting a new convert to the Mormon faith. Curiosity then led him to investigate the faith of the man he had defended, and he was converted and baptized in 1841. He arrived in Nauvoo in the spring of 1843.

He soon became a member of the Nauvoo Legion and the Nauvoo Brass Band. As a singer, he became a special favorite of the Prophet Joseph Smith and was often called upon to sing for important visitors to Nauvoo. It was a special pleasure of the Prophet to hear John Kay sing the dramatic piece performed by baritones through the years, "The sea, the sea, the open sea!" Following the martyrdom, John Taylor wrote new words, "The seer, the seer, Joseph the seer!" On December 26, 1844, only six months after the martyrdom, the Seventies Hall was dedicated in Nauvoo, with an inspiring program under the direction of Brigham Young. One of the memorable highlights was the singing by John Kay of "The Seer, the Seer, Joseph the Seer!"[3]

John Kay's singing was an important factor in the popularity of the band, headed by William Pitt, in the journey across Iowa and into Winter Quarters. Then, as the city on the Missouri began to take shape, the band played for every important occasion.

John left to spend the winter with George Miller's company,

more than a hundred miles west of Winter Quarters, but on March 6, he returned to the main Camp of Israel, suffering from frozen feet and privation. With a firm display of special fellowship, the members of William Pitt's band played a series of concerts, secured donations of cash and provisions, and helped restore John to health and activity.

Elder Kay was to stay in Winter Quarters for another year, helping to cheer the thousands who would not leave for the new Zion until 1848. However, he left for the Salt Lake Valley with Brigham Young's company. His last service to migrating Saints came in 1864 when, returning from a mission to his native England, he was placed in charge of a large group of British converts aboard the sailing vessel *Hudson*. The voyage was a perilous one, and ten Saints lost their lives at sea. On the overland journey to Salt Lake City, Elder Kay died. On the evening of his death, he seemed to rouse from his fever and stood in the door of his tent, singing the songs he had sung through the years to cheer the hearts of weary travelers.[4]

A dominant figure in the music of the migrating Saints was the bandleader and musician William Pitt. At his funeral services in Salt Lake City, February 23, 1873, Wilford Woodruff gave an outpouring of affection for this man of music. William Pitt was a member of the vast harvest of souls in Herefordshire, England, when Wilford Woodruff served his first mission there. In William's funeral eulogy, Wilford told how men of the congregation William had abandoned surrounded the building where the Latter-day Saints were gathered. Yelling and throwing stones, they broke every window in the upper story of the building and left the rooms strewn with broken glass. When Wilford Woodruff decided to go out and confront the attackers, he was restrained by William Pitt who himself opened the door and walked into the stone-throwing crowd. He simply took down the names of all the men he knew among the assailants. They stoned him back into the house, but they soon left the scene. As Wilford Woodruff recalled: "It was one of Brother Pitt's first labors with me, and I will say that, from that time to the present day, he has been a true and faithful servant of God and of his Church."

The apostle told of another incident that cemented William Pitt's relationship to the Latter-day Saints. William's sister, Mary Pitt, was an invalid. For fourteen years, she had been unable to walk, and for half of that time, she had been bedfast. When she requested baptism and the healing of her illness, Wilford Woodruff asked if she had faith that she would be healed. The assurance seemed complete. Soon Brigham Young and Willard Richards arrived at the scene and the three united in administering the ordinance of healing. Describing the incident Wilford Woodruff said: "She laid down her crutch and never used it after, and the next day she walked three miles." The healing was the talk of the area, and conversions to the Church continued.

Other speakers at the funeral included John Taylor, who had also been present at the amazing expansion of the work in the British Mission. Then came Daniel H. Wells, Second Counselor to President Brigham Young. His memorial tribute shows the influence of William Pitt on two generations of Latter-day Saints:

> I have been associated with Brother Pitt a good many years. He taught music in my family as early, I think as 1842, and I have been intimately associated with him in the public works, in the Legion, and in the band he has led, and I have never seen that man when he was not cheerful and full of life. Indeed, I have thought he had more music in him than any man I have ever known. If there was a musical instrument he could not play, I do not know what it is. He was always faithful and cheerful under the most trying circumstances, and no matter what blast blew of difficulty or persecution, Brother Pitt was there on hand at a moment's notice, full of life and music, ready to cheer the hearts of the people.
>
> He was a beautiful painter, and followed that trade for subsistence. He was always industrious and ready to do a job of work, whether or not he could get anything for it. It made no difference; it was for the kingdom, and it was all right. He was one of the best of men in my opinion, and, as has been said, it is well with him.
>
> I suppose there are a great many here who would like to bear testimony and speak a good word for Brother Pitt; but, brethren, he does not need it—his whole life has spoken for itself and will speak eternally.[5]

Inspired direction, devotion to duty, and belief in a cause beyond the present contributed to the success of the Mormon migration, but the music that kept hearts light and souls focused on eternal purpose played a major part. By the Winter Quarters period, the Latter-day Saints had accumulated an impressive hymnody. The Church was but three months old when the Prophet Joseph Smith delivered a revelation to his wife, Emma. Hailing her as an elect lady, the revelation called upon her to accomplish many things. It instructed: "Make a selection of sacred hymns, as it shall be given thee, which is pleasing unto me, to be had in my Church. For my soul delighteth in the song of the heart; yea, the song of the righteous is a prayer unto me, and it shall be answered with a blessing upon their heads."[6]

During the next two years, Emma evidently worked hard at her assignment, and on May 1, 1832, she received important help. William W. Phelps was called to correct and print the hymns that had been selected by Emma Smith. At the same time, William W. Phelps was directed, with the assistance of Oliver Cowdery and John Whitmer, to print three thousand copies of the Book of Commandments, the foundation for the Doctrine and Covenants, now one of the standard scriptures of the Church.[7]

W. W. Phelps came to his position as printer and editor with a wealth of experience. He was editing a newspaper, the *Ontario Phoenix*, an anti-Masonic paper, at the time when the conflict over Masonry was a dominant factor in New York state politics. Active politically, he was once considered as a candidate for lieutenant governor on the anti-Masonic party. In 1830, Parley P. Pratt, in one of his early missionary efforts, presented W. W. Phelps with a copy of the Book of Mormon. It had the same electrifying effect upon W. W. Phelps that Parley P. Pratt himself had so recently felt. In December 1830, W. W. Phelps met the Prophet for the first time. This encounter led to a dramatic change in the life of William Wines Phelps. He later wrote: "When I for the first time held a conversation with our beloved brother, Joseph, who I was willing to acknowledge as a prophet of the Lord, and to whose godly account of himself and the work he was engaged in, I owe my first determination to quit the folly of my way and the fancy and fame of this world and seek the Lord in his righteousness in order to enter a better world."[8]

On May 11, 1831, he published his final issue of the *Ontario Phoenix*, announcing his intention to offer his time and talents "to the upbuilding of the Kingdom of God upon earth." Then he loaded his family in a carriage and headed for Kirtland, Ohio, where the Prophet and the entire Church had moved from New York. He arrived just in time to learn of a projected move farther west. Joseph asked the Lord for guidance concerning the newly arrived W. W. Phelps and was given a revelation directed to William. He was directed to be baptized and to be ordained an elder, and to "preach repentance and remission of sins by way of baptism in the name of Jesus Christ the son of the living God." He was also called to assist Oliver Cowdery in the work of printing and writing books for schools in the Church. The revelation also instructed: "Take your journey with my servants, Joseph Smith, Junior, and Sidney Rigdon, that you may be planted in the land of your inheritance to do this work."

A month later, July 1831, another revelation in Independence, Missouri, enlarged W. W. Phelps's calling. It said:

> Let my servant William W. Phelps be planted in this place, and be established as a printer unto the Church.
> And lo, if the world receive his writings—behold here in wisdom—let him obtain whatsoever he can in righteousness for the good of the Saints.
> And let my servant Oliver Cowdery assist him, even as I have commanded, in whatsoever place I shall appoint him, to copy and to correct and select, that all things may be right before me, as it should be proved by my spirit through him.[9]

Thus did the former New York editor find himself established in a printing shop in the bustling frontier town of Independence. Here he published a newspaper, the *Evening and Morning Star*, devoted principally to the interests of the Church. Here, also, he began setting the type for the Book of Commandments and the first Latter-day Saint hymnbook.

It was the newspaper that brought disaster upon his enterprise. In 1833, Missouri was already a battleground between factions on the subject of slavery. In late June, W. W. Phelps published a seemingly harmless editorial on the subject "Free People of Color," but the mere headline was sufficient to stir up passions. An "extra" by the *Star* on July 2 failed to correct the damage, and a committee asked Editor Phelps to close down the paper and leave the county. The Brethren asked for time to consider the demands; this was denied and a mob descended upon the printing office, destroyed the press and all of the carefully set type, and leveled the building to the ground. Two of the Phelps children were buried in the rubble but later rescued. The attack upon the press was but the beginning of the violence that drove the Saints from Jackson County.[10]

W. W. Phelps led the exodus to Clay County, but soon, at the Prophet's request, found himself back in Kirtland, Ohio, compiling the first edition of the newly entitled Doctrine and Covenants. He also assisted Emma Smith with the compiling and publication of the interrupted hymnbook.[11]

Entitled *A Collection of Sacred Hymns for the Church of Jesus Christ of Latter-day Saints, selected by Emma Smith*, the publication was a pocket-sized volume of ninety hymns, the words only. In many cases, searchers have been unable to ascertain to what tunes they were originally sung, but many were well-known and cherished Protestant hymns. Some of these are so much a part of Mormon hymnology today that we may be surprised to learn they had other origins. For example: "I Know That My Redeemer Lives," by Samuel Medley, and "Arise, My Soul, Arise," from Wesley's collection.

But there were also many hymns that were strictly Latter-day Saint, hailing the restoration and presenting principles of revealed doctrine. Parley P. Pratt, who headed the first mission to the Lamanites on the western frontier, wrote: "Oh, stop and tell me, red man, who are you, why you roam." The most poetic of the early Latter-day Saints, Eliza R. Snow, wrote "Great Is the Lord" and "The Glorious Day Is Rolling On." Bishop Edward Partridge hailed the coming of a new Zion with "Let Zion in Her Beauty Rise."[12]

Most of all, there was W. W. Phelps. He not only assisted Emma Smith with selecting and compiling the hymns, he personally wrote the words to twenty-nine of the ninety. Ten of them have survived and are sung by Mormons in many languages. The hymnbook was less than a year old when the Kirtland Temple was dedicated. For W. W. Phelps it was a time of glory. Immediately after the dedicatory prayer, a choir sang his song "The Spirit of God Like a Fire is Burning." *History of the Church* lists the tune as "Hosannah," but modern tune detectives have sought in vain for the origin. Where William W. Phelps encountered the melody that has been sung through the years and has been heard at the dedication of temples and chapels for a century and a half, is still a mystery. He was not a musician, but he had the ability to remember tunes to which his words might be set. Another of his hymns, which was sung at the dedication, is "Now, Let Us Rejoice in the Day of Salvation." Its melody has the spirit of a camp meeting waltz song, but again, its origin is a mystery. At least four W. W. Phelps hymns were sung during the three-day dedication, and he was among those who testified that angels were indeed "coming to visit the earth," and that he saw and heard them within the walls of the Kirtland Temple.[13]

Others of W. W. Phelps's hymns include "Praise to the Man," "Redeemer of Israel," and "Gently Raise the Sacred Strain."

William W. Phelps had a stormy and erratic life. After the triumphant experiences at Kirtland, he was back in Missouri. He found himself in alliance against the Prophet Joseph Smith and was excommunicated from the Church. His letter of repentance and the words of the Prophet, welcoming him back to the fold, are prime examples of the spirit of repentance and forgiveness.[14] W. W. Phelps was again a foremost worker in the cause. At Winter Quarters, he set out on an important mission, to buy a printing press to be carried by the Church to its new headquarters in the West. The press was secured and would print the first issues of the *Deseret News* in the new Zion. But on the trip, W. W. Phelps again fell into transgression and was excommunicated by Brigham Young and the Quorum of the Twelve.[15]

Again, there was repentance, forgiveness and rebaptism, and in 1848, he was on his way to Utah. There, he was cofounder and chancellor of the University of Deseret, helped to write the constitution for the Provisional State of Deseret, and served for years in the Utah Territorial Legislature.[16] All these will be remembered, but none with more pleasure or importance than the hymns he wrote to remind Latter-day Saints of their heritage.

That the Latter-day Saints were a hymn-singing people is demonstrated by the many hymnbooks that followed the first. An 1838 edition was published in New York by David W. Rogers. It was the first to contain Parley P. Pratt's great hymn of the restoration, "An Angel from on High." An 1839 edition, published by Benjamin C. Ellsworth, contained 114 hymns. A larger and more important compilation was made in Great Britain in 1840. It was selected by Brigham Young, John Taylor, and Parley P. Pratt. It contained 217 hymns, with Parley P. Pratt and Eliza R. Snow among the authors of added hymns. In this collection was a poignant English song entitled "A Poor Wayfaring Man of Grief." The song became popular in Nauvoo before the martyrdom, and in Carthage Jail, Joseph Smith asked John Taylor to sing it for him. The most recent hymnbook in the hands of the Saints at Winter Quarters was the edition printed in Nauvoo in 1841 by Ebenezer Robinson.[17]

As important as the stirring strains of band music or the quiet comfort of hymns was the music that set toes a tapping as the Saints danced their way across the plains. At a time when many religious bodies considered all dancing to be sinful, Brigham Young proclaimed it as an act of worship. Before the dedication of the Nauvoo Temple, at the close of a hard day's work in finishing the structure, President Young authorized dancing in the temple "to enliven the spirits of the Saints."[18] They danced to celebrate the marriage of Heber C. Kimball's daughter, Helen, to Horace K. Whitney. In her diary, she recalled the many hardships and recounted the joy dancing could bring. She wrote: "But there was no mourning nor lamentations; we felt too glad to make our escape; and the first evening after the warm sun had dried the earth, the young people were out dancing by moonlight—determined upon being happy, or at least to snatch all the pleasant moments and enjoy them as they came along."[19]

Church historian Andrew Jenson compiled from journals of the time a "Manuscript History of Winter Quarters." The day-by-day records are filled with music and dancing. On October 1, 1846, Horace K. Whitney recorded that he, with several of the boys, was engaged in haying, and in the evening he played the violin at a party on the anniversary of his little sister Maria's birthday. On October 3, he mentioned a band that played at Winter Quarters. He wrote: "I joined them and played with them. I am to use the flute formerly played by Andrew Cahoon who expects to start shortly for England." On November 12, he wrote: "Brother Kimball, Bishop Miller and myself went to Brigham's house, which is just finished, in honor of which we spent the evening in dancing."

On New Year's eve, 1846, Helen Mar Whitney wrote: "This evening, Brother Kimball again gave up his room for the purpose of dancing. Brigham and some of his family were present, besides a numerous assembly of brethren and sisters. This evening, like the Christmas one, passed off finely under the direction of Orrin Porter Rockwell, and every one departed to their homes about one o'clock A.M., apparently well pleased and gratified with our scene of festivity."

By February, the new Council House had been completed, and Helen Whitney wrote: "The Bishops' convivialities commenced at the Council House today under the direction of Bishop Newel K. Whitney as head Bishop of the Church. Horace K. Whitney attended with the band and played. The day and evening passed off finely, spent in singing, praying, dancing, etc."[20]

For many of the Saints this would be the last festivity in the

Council House, for they were preparing to leave for the mountains as soon as spring came. Brigham Young had received approval from the High Councils of the Church for the revelation, "The Word and Will of the Lord, at the Winter Quarters of the Camp of Israel," and had distributed it to the people. Father John Smith, uncle of the Prophet, was busy giving Patriarchal Blessings to those preparing for the journey. But the Patriarch was also the head of an organization of the community's elderly, the "Silver Grays." The group planned a dance at the Council House and invited the Quorum of the Twelve and other leaders to attend.[21] In his journal, Brigham Young felt the need of some comments on the subject of dancing. He wrote:

> Nothing will infringe more upon the traditions of some men than to dance. Infidels dance, also the wicked, the vain, foolish, giddy and those that know not God. There is no harm in dancing. The Lord said he wanted His saints to praise Him in all things. It was enjoined on Miriam and the daughters of Israel to dance and celebrate the name of the Almighty, and to praise him on the destruction of Pharaoh and his host.
>
> For some weeks past I could not wake up at any time of the night but I heard the axe at work. Some were building for the destitute and the widow; and now my feelings are, dance all night if you desire to do so, for there is no harm in it. The prayer of the wicked is an abomination in the sight of God, but it is not a sin for a saint to pray; where there is no evil intended, there is no sin. I enjoin upon the Bishops that they gather the widow, the poor and the fatherless together and remember them in the festivities of Israel.
>
> Patriarch John Smith made some comforting remarks and exhorted the brethren and sisters to dance, sing, and enjoy themselves the best way they could. The center of the floor was then cleared for the dance when the Silver Grays and spectacled dames enjoyed themselves in the dance; it was indeed an interesting novel sight, to behold the old men and women, some nearly a hundred years old, dancing like ancient Israel.[22]

Music and dance was indeed an important part of Winter Quarters. Some notes from the "Manuscript History of Winter Quarters" indicate the scope of this activity:

> Wednesday, January 12, 1848. At this time, Hiram Gates had four hundred scholars attending his dancing school at Winter Quarters. Classes met from 10 A.M. to 3 P.M. and from 4 P.M. to 9 P.M.
>
> Sunday, January 30. A select committee met at Winter Quarters for the purpose of making arrangements for a festival for those who were actively engaged in the battle of Nauvoo in 1846. The festival took place February 3.

Tuesday, February 1. The people of Winter Quarters during the previous month had several picnic parties in the Council House. The dancing classes of Hiram Gates also contributed much to the cheerfulness of the community amid the hardships and privations to which they were exposed.

Saturday, Feb 5. A meeting of the Second Quorum of Seventy was held at Winter Quarters. Heber C. Kimball, Joseph Young and other prominent men were present. The day was spent in preaching, singing, music, dancing and feasting. An abundance of pies, sweet cakes, home made beer, etc. was served.

March 14. Hiram Gates reported 440 pupils in his dancing school.

Chapter Eight

WE'LL FIND THE PLACE

A place of refuge in the Rocky Mountains had found its place in the dreams of members of The Church of Jesus Christ of Latter-day Saints even before it became certain they would be driven from their thriving city of Nauvoo. On August 6, 1842, Joseph Smith uttered a prophecy that has not found its way into the Church's official record of prophecies, the Doctrine and Covenants. On that day, Joseph, with a number of other brethren, crossed the Mississippi into Montrose, Iowa, to witness the installation of new officers of the Rising Star Lodge, Ancient York Masons. The Prophet recorded the event:

> I had a conversation with a number of brethren in the shade of the building on the subject of our persecutions in Missouri, and the constant annoyance which has followed us since we were driven from that state. I prophesied that the Saints would continue to suffer much affliction and would be driven to the Rocky Mountains; many would apostatize, others would be put to death by our persecutors or lose their lives in consequence of exposure or disease, and some of you will live to go and assist in building settlements and build cities and see the Saints become a mighty people in the midst of the Rocky Mountains.[1]

Years later, in an affidavit, Anson Call remembered that prophesy. He said:

> Joseph, who was with us, told us of many things which would transpire in the mountains. After drinking a drought of ice water, he said, "Brethren, this water tastes much like the crystal streams that are running in the Rocky Mountains which some of you will participate of. There are some of those standing here that will perform a great work in that land," pointing to Shadrach Roundy and a number of others whom I have forgotten. "There is Anson. He shall go and shall assist in building cities from one end of the country to the other, and you shall perform as great a work as has ever been done by man, so that the nations of the earth shall be astonished and many of these will be gathered to that land and in assisting in building cities and temples

and Israel shall be made to rejoice, but before you see this day, you will pass through scenes that are but little understood by you. This people will be made to mourn, multitudes will die and many will apostatize, but the Priesthood shall prevail over all its enemies, triumph over the devil, never more to be thrown down."[2]

The Prophet's interest in the Rocky Mountains and all the lands that led to them continued to be active the following year. In July 1843, he called upon Jonathan Dunham to lead an exploring expedition into the Indian country of Iowa. Dunham, himself of Indian extraction, made a complete report of this expedition, which the Prophet entered into his *History of the Church*. Jonathan spent two weeks struggling through Iowa, in weather that should have prepared the Saints for what they would experience three years later. He reached the chief village of the Pottawatomie Indians on the east bank of the Missouri River on July 29. He spent two weeks with this tribe, sharing their food, learning their customs, and gaining their favor. When the time came for him to return to Nauvoo, the Pottawatomie chief chose an escort to protect and guide him. It took them but eight days to cross Iowa into Nauvoo.[3]

Dunham's expedition may well have been inspired by a visit to the Prophet, on July 2, by several Pottawatomie chiefs. They told the Prophet of their sufferings and that they had come a long way to see him and hear his words. As reported by Wilford Woodruff, Joseph Smith told them the following:

> The Great Spirit has told you the truth. I am your friend and brother and will do you good. Your fathers were once a great people. They worshipped the Great Spirit. The Great Spirit did them good. He was their friend, but they left the Great Spirit and would not hear his words or keep them. The Great Spirit left them, and they began to kill one another, and they have been poor and afflicted until now.
> The Great Spirit has given me a book, and told me that you will soon be blessed again. . . . This is the book which your fathers made. I wrote upon it (showing them the Book of Mormon.) This tells you what you will have to do. I now want you to begin to pray to the Great Spirit. I want you to make peace with one another, and do not kill any more Indians; it is not good. Do not kill white men; it is not good; but ask the Great Spirit for what you want, and it will not be long before the Great Spirit will bless you, and you will cultivate the earth and build good houses like white men.[4]

Good relations with the Indians were essential for any major westward migration, and Joseph was pursuing the subject vigorously. Jonathan Dunham's report was digested thoroughly by the Prophet, and in February 1844, he was ready to propose a larger exploration. On February 21, a meeting of the Twelve was called. Brigham Young, President of the Quorum, and six other members were present. In a summons to the Quorum on the previous day, Joseph outlined his purpose:

> I instructed the Twelve Apostles to send out a delegation and investigate the locations of California and Oregon, and hunt out a good location, where we can remove to, after the temple is completed, and where we can build a city in a day, and have a government of our own, get up into the mountains, where the devil cannot dig us out, and live in a healthful climate, where we can live as old as we have a mind to.

When the Quorum met on the 21st, they already had some volunteers for the exploration. Jonathan Dunham was first on the list, along with Phineas H. Young, David D. Yearsley, and David Fullmer. Four others were requested to join them, and all were to be notified to appear before the Quorum the following Friday. Joseph reported the proceedings of that meeting:

> I told them I wanted an exploration of all that mountain country. Perhaps it would be best to go direct to Santa Fe. Send twenty five men; let them preach the gospel wherever they go. Let that man go that can raise $500, a good horse and mule, a double-barrel gun, one barrel rifle and the other smooth bore, a saddle and a bridle, a pair of revolving pistols, bowie-knife and a good sabre. Appoint a leader and let them beat up for volunteers.[5]

With that meeting, it may have appeared that the exploration of the West was almost under way, but the tide of events was sweeping the plans before it. A few days earlier, Joseph Smith had announced his candidacy for President of the United States. Before the spring was over, apostasy from within and persecution from without brought the Prophet and other Church leaders into a series of legal actions that would culminate in the martyrdom of the Prophet.

On April 24, 1845, Jonathan Dunham, with four other elders, set out from Nauvoo westward, on another mission to the Lamanites. On September 1, Elders Daniel Spencer and Charles Shumway, returning from that same mission, reported that Elder Jonathan Dunham had died on July 28, 1845, "a little before daylight."[6]

When Brigham Young and his Camp of Israel set off across Iowa from Nauvoo in February 1846, they could have used the pioneering knowledge of Jonathan Dunham and his Indian friends. It took Brigham's company nearly six months to negotiate the distance covered by Jonathan in eight days. Still, the vision of reaching the Rocky Mountains that same year burned brightly. As late as July 17, Brigham Young was talking about "a company to go over the mountains." Two weeks later, events had forced him to change his plans. On August 1, he wrote to George Miller, encamped a hundred and fifty miles westward:

> Dear Brother Miller and Captain of Fifties, Greeting:
>   The Council of the Twelve, with about three hundred wagons, are now encamped about four miles west of the Missouri River and scores of wagons are still crossing. The health of the camp on this side of the river is generally good. On the other side, considerable sickness prevails. . . .
>   Above five hundred of our brethren have volunteered in the U. S. service for California. They were marched from here some few days since, all in good spirits; this has left us quite destitute of men to manage our flocks and teams. . . .
>   We think it would be wisdom for as many teams and Saints among your companies to winter at the Pawnee village as can well be sustained, the balance to winter at Grand Island or nearby, and in the spring we will overtake you and all cross to the mountains together.[7]

The call of the Mormon Battalion had served as a valuable reason for halting the westward march at the Missouri. It had taken six months to travel three hundred miles, and an unknown thousand mile stretch of plains and mountains lay before them. The move into Winter Quarters would afford a time to study the accumulated information about the western lands, to gather new information, and to make more thorough preparations for the migration in the spring.

A winter's resting place would also give the Church the opportunity to give renewed emphasis to foreign missionary work. On the very day that President Young wrote to George Miller, three members of the Quorum of the Twelve (Orson Hyde, Parley P. Pratt, and John Taylor) set out on the Missouri for a trip to England. It was a long and hazardous journey, but in mid-October they had arrived in Great Britain, and the work of the British Mission would continue its phenomenal growth.[8] Soon missions would be formed in Europe and throughout much of the world. The trails that were being planned at Winter Quarters would be filled with immigrants to Zion for many years to come.

On Sunday, August 9, the Saints assembled on the west bank of the Missouri and met for a worship service in a hastily prepared open air meeting place. Some three hundred were present. Brigham Young confided that he had not really "expected to see the Rocky

Mountains this year." Then he added, "Whenever the Lord com-
mands me to go, I expect to start."

On that same evening, the remaining members of the Quorum
of the Twelve met and heard clerk Willard Richards read the text
of a letter that President Young had just written to President James
K. Polk of the United States, explaining again the reasons for the
exile of the Mormons to the western boundaries of the country
and into Indian territory.

Geography of the proposed home in the West was beginning
to take shape, and Brigham saw it as a place "where a good living
[would] require hard labor, and consequently [would] be coveted
by no other people, while it is surrounded by so unpopulous but
fertile country."[9]

The Saints knew that their travels would be through Indian
territory, and that their relations to the natives would be crucial
to the success of every journey. Mormon leaders wanted every
Indian tribe along the way to know that the Mormons were their
friends. Behind the amazing success of the Mormons in dealing
with the Indians through the years is a firm religious doctrine as
to who the Indians are. The Saints in Winter Quarters had a song
written by Parley P. Pratt in their latest hymnbook:

> On, stop and tell me red man
> Who are you, why you roam,
> And how you make your living,
> Have you no God, no home?
>
> I once was pleasant Ephraim
> When Jacob for me prayed,
> But, oh, how joys all vanish
> When man from God has strayed![10]

The Indians had a warm community of interest with the Mormons. Both had suffered persecution and had been driven from
their homes because their way of life was different. On the way
to Winter Quarters, at Mount Pisgah, Chief Pied Riche of the
Pottawatomie tribe told the leaders of the Camp of Israel how his
own people had been driven from their former homeland in Michigan. He was quoted as saying: "We must help one another, and
the Great Spirit will help us both. Because one suffers and does
not deserve it is no reason he shall suffer always. We may live to
see it right yet."[11]

After the move to the west side of the Missouri, Brigham Young found a similar spirit of human brotherhood among the Omahas, despite some misunderstandings and considerable theft by younger braves of the tribe. He quotes Omaha Chief Big Elk as saying:

> We heard you were a good people; we are glad to have you come and keep a store where we can buy things cheap. You can stay with us while we hold these lands, but we expect to sell as our Grandfather will buy. We will likely move northward.
>
> While you are among us as brethren, we will be brethren to you. I like, my son, what you have said very well. It could be said no better by anyone.[12]

There would be frequent conferences and many disagreements among the Mormon leaders, the Omaha chiefs, and the Indian agents assigned to the area by the United States government, but the general outcome was favorable relations with the Indians. Brigham Young took the further precautions of making sure that the President of the United States was aware of the Church's attitude toward the natives. On September 9, 1846, he wrote President Polk. In part, the letter read as follows:

> Since our communication of the 9th ult. to your excellency, the Omaha Indians have returned from their council with their chiefs and braves, who expressed a willingness that we should tarry on their lands, and use what wood and timber would be necessary for our convenience while we are preparing to prosecute our journey, as may be seen from a duplicate of theirs to us, as of the 31st of August, which will be presented by Colonel Kane.
>
> In Council, they were much more specific than in their writings, and Big Elk, in behalf of his nation, requested us to lend them teams to draw their corn at harvest, and help them keep it after it was deposited, to assist them in building houses, making fields, doing some blacksmithing, etc., etc., and to teach some of their young men to do the same, and also keep some goods and trade with them while we tarried among them.
>
> We responded to all their wishes in the same spirit of kindness manifested by them, and told them we would do them all the good we could, with the same provision they made "if the President is willing," which is why we write.[13]

In the same letter, President Young advised the president of the presence of George Miller's encampment to the west among the Ponca Indians.

As President of the Quorum of the Twelve, Brigham Young gave frequent advice to his people concerning relations with the Indians. They were to respect the Indians' religious beliefs and burial customs. President Young said: "Disturb no Indian grave.

Because the Indians frequently deposit their dead in the branches of trees, wrapt in buffalo robes and blankets, leaving with them arrows, pipe and other trinkets, which they consider sacred, and we should not remove them, and our children should be taught to leave them alone."

Again, he told a meeting of the High Council: "We should not invite the Indians to our camp; we could go and see them. We want the privilege of staying on their land this winter, cutting timber, building houses, perhaps leaving some families and crops. We might do them good by repairing their guns, learning them how and teaching their children. . . . They should not touch our property and we will not theirs."[14]

There would be violations of that understanding, on both sides, but they were minimal. The careful and patient cultivation of better relations with the native tribes would bring rewards over the many years of Mormon migration. No other migration of comparable magnitude passed through the Indian lands with so great a success.

The Indians proved a vital source of information on the country through which the Saints traveled, and Mormon leaders took every opportunity to increase the contacts with various tribes. Brigham Young's *Manuscript History* shows many contacts with Logan Fontenelle, an Indian interpreter. Orson Pratt was sent on a brief mission to the Otoe Indians, to gather information and to settle differences between that tribe and the Omahas. All of these contacts would increase the knowledge about the final place of refuge for the Camp of Israel, and the routes they should take to their destination.

By the winter of 1846-47, in Winter Quarters, Brigham Young accumulated many materials about the West, most probably Lansford W. Hastings' *Emigrants Guide to Oregon and California*, which was published in 1845, and by the following year had swept the country as almost a bible to emigrants heading westward.[15] The guide, however, proved grossly inaccurate a year after its publication.

Winter was coming early, and on November 24, ice was floating down the Missouri. Saints could be thankful for homes, however primitive, and warm fires. They could not have known that on that very date members of the tragic Donner Party were dying of cold and hunger in the deep snows of the high Sierras.

On that November 24, President Brigham Young received two

visitors. One was Justin Groselande, a trader for the American Fur Company. His companion was a Mr. Cardenale. Mr. Groselande was a trader among the Crow Indians and had lived among various Indian tribes of the far west for some sixteen years. Horace H. Whitney's account of the meeting says the men had lived in the Salt Lake area for much of that period and told their experiences to President Young. The visitors made an offer. They would be at liberty next season and would pilot the camp over the mountains for a fee of two hundred dollars. For another two hundred, Mr. Cardenale would go along and hunt game. That evening, Heber C. Kimball was called in to confer with the visitors.

The next day was still icy cold, and the visitors continued their conference. Their offer to escort the migration was not accepted, but John Kay and Samuel Gully were assigned to escort them to Bishop George Miller's camp. The visitors had sketched maps of the western region and added still more to Brigham Young's knowledge of where the Saints were going and how to get there.[16]

Throughout the winter, Church leaders sought every opportunity to further their studies of the Rocky Mountain area. Perhaps the most important visitor was Father Pierre Jean De Smet, a Catholic priest who had lived among the Blackfoot Indians for many years, and who had explored the Salt Lake Valley in 1841. How much influence he had on the Mormon leader is unknown, but historian B. H. Roberts quotes a letter Father De Smet wrote to De Smet's nephew in 1851:

> In the fall of 1846, as I drew near to the frontiers of the state of Missouri, I found the advance guard of the Mormons, numbering about 10,000, camped on the territory of the Omahas, not far from the old Council Bluffs. They had just been driven out for a second time from a state of the union. (Illinois had received them after their war with the people of Missouri.) They had resolved to winter on the threshold of the great desert, and then to move westward into it, to put distance between them and their persecutors, without even knowing at that time the end of their long wanderings, nor the place where they should erect permanent dwellings. They asked me a thousand questions about the regions I had explored and the valley which I have just described to you pleased them greatly from the account I gave them of it. Was that what determined them? I would not dare to assert it. They are there! In the last three years, Utah has changed its aspect, and from a desert has become a flourishing territory, which will soon become one of the states of the union.[17]

Father De Smet's question may never be properly answered. B. H. Roberts gave the opinion that the Mormon leaders already knew where they were going. Certainly the pioneering Catholic priest helped to confirm their choice, perhaps even to locate more definitely the exact geographical location.

As 1846 drew to its close, Brigham Young was consolidating his information. The Church historian prepared a year-end report on the condition of the Camp of Israel, and on January 1, the members of the Quorum of the Twelve drew up an extended report to its three members in England: Orson Hyde, Parley Pratt, and John Taylor. The report stated:

> Our great city, which sprang up in a night, as it were, like Jonah's gourd, is divided into twenty-two wards, over which twenty-two Bishops with their councilors preside, and no one suffers for food or raiment unless it be through their own fault; that is, in not asking for it, or being well and too lazy to work, for the fact of so many houses having been built in so short a time is a proof of the general industry of the people, which will bear comparison with the history of all the nations of the earth, and in all periods of time.

After detailing more information about the city, the progress in building a flour mill and a council house, the report turned to plans for the future, as discussed in a three-day meeting at Christmas time. It said:

> The main subject was left to our Council, with the general impression that the pioneer company of some two to three hundred, more or less, would be fitted out as soon as circumstances would possibly permit, so as to be at the foot of the mountains, somewhere in the region of the Yellowstone River, perhaps at the fork of the Tongue River, say two days ride north of the Oregon Road, and a week's travel west of Fort Laramie, with plows, corn, beans, etc., prepared to raise a summer crop, for some thousand or two of the Saints who should follow after them as soon as grazing would permit.

It is difficult to find any correlation between these plans and the route the pioneers took. On January 14, 1847, Brigham reported in his journal: "I commenced to give the Word and Will of God concerning the emigration of the Saints and those who journey with them." He worked far into the night, dictating the words to Dr. Willard Richards in the Octagon House. The next day, the Quorum of the Twelve met at Elder Ezra T. Benson's house and decided that "the Word and Will of the Lord" should be laid before the Councils of the Church. It was next presented to the Municipal High Council, who approved it unanimously and enthusiastically. The Councils of Seventies and High Priests were equally unanimous, and on Sunday the 17th, a general meeting of the Church

gave unanimous support to the only revelation from God ever announced by Brigham Young. They were not proclaimed as his words,
but the words of the God of Israel. Pondering over their acceptance
by all of his people, Brigham Young wrote: "I had no more doubts
nor fears of going to the mountains and felt as much security as
if I possessed the treasures of the East."[18]

The document speaks for itself. It became the guide for twenty-
two years of emigration, until the coming of the railroads to the
West in 1869. It has become Latter-day Saint scripture as section
136 of the Doctrine and Covenants. Of all the travelers to the
American West, none had a comparable statement of purpose to
guide them. It states:

> The Word and Will of the Lord concerning the Camp of Israel in
> their journeyings to the West:
> Let all the people of the Church of Jesus Christ of Latter-day Saints,
> and those who journey with them, be organized into companies, with
> a covenant and promise to keep all the commandments and statutes
> of the Lord our God.
> Let the companies be organized with captains of hundreds, captains
> of fifties and captains of tens, with a president and his two councilors
> at their head, under the direction of the Twelve Apostles.
> And this shall be our covenant – that we will walk in all the ordi-
> nances of the Lord.

The revelation outlined responsibility for providing wagons
and teams, decisions as to how many should migrate in the current
season, and who should stay to build wagons and produce crops
to feed those who would migrate and those who would stay. The
document contains only forty-two verses, but they are filled with
immediate instructions and long-range principles.

An important feature of the revelation was the clear statement
that the Twelve Apostles were to be in charge of the migrations.
Years earlier, a Council of Fifty, containing both members and
nonmembers of the Church, was organized to plan the westward
move. The Municipal Councils, of Nauvoo and then of Winter
Quarters, had their parts in the decisions. Now, clearly, the
Quorum of the Twelve would be in control.

Organization of the pioneer company was soon moving rapidly.
Almost every day, Brigham's journal contained references to the
appointment of captains of hundreds, fifties and tens, of company
leaders and councilors. Soon the decision would have to be made
as to the composition of that first company of pioneers, those who
would find the place that God had prepared for them, there to

plant crops to sustain the Saints through their first winter in the Rocky Mountains. By the end of March 1847, the personnel of this select group had all been chosen. Twenty-five pioneers said they were ready to go immediately and another thirty-two within a few days.[19]

There were 148 persons in that first pioneer company: 143 men, 3 women, and 2 children. Eight of the Twelve Apostles were included. Lyman Wight, although still holding his membership in the quorum, had left the main body of the Church before the exodus from Nauvoo and had already led a body of his followers into Texas. The other three members had been filling urgent missionary duties in Great Britain and returned to Winter Quarters just in time to bid the pioneers farewell. Orson Hyde was placed in charge of the Saints on both sides of the Missouri during the absence of the leaders. John Taylor and Parley P. Pratt formed their own companies, including many newly arrived Saints, to leave Winter Quarters in early summer.[20]

William Clayton's services as clerk and secretary were valuable on the trip. Such rugged frontiersmen as Howard Egan and Orrin Porter Rockwell proved their worth in breaking trails, fording rivers, and providing protection from the Indians. Appleton Harmon was a skilled mechanic. Hans Christian Hansen, a Danish convert, was an excellent violinist and his mastery of the instrument provided many happy hours at campgrounds along the way. Another musician, a young Irishman named James Craig, found himself assigned as the bugler of the pioneers. Orson Pratt was the chief surveyor and scientist of the company, and Thomas Bullock served as secretary and historian.[21]

The choice of the three women and two children as members of the pioneer company must have caused conflicts and disappointments. Of the several wives of Brigham Young, he took only one with him, the youngest, Clarissa Decker Young, who would reach her nineteenth birthday as the first Saints were entering Salt Lake Valley. Her favored place is explained by her niece, Clarissa Young Spencer, whose mother, Lucy Decker Young, was another of Brigham's wives:

> Aunt Clara Decker, Mother's own younger sister, was the wife who accompanied Father in the first company of 143 pioneers who blazed the trail into the Salt Lake Valley for the great number who were to come later. Because of this, she is often called "the pioneer wife." At first, it had been thought wisest to take only men upon this

arduous journey, since not even their exact destination had fully been decided upon; but as Heber C. Kimball was not very well at the time, it was necessary for his wife to go with him. Of course, she did not care to be the only woman in the company, so two others came as well, Clara and her mother, Harriett Page Decker Young, who was at that time the wife of Father's brother, Lorenzo Young. My mother and Aunt Clara were, of course, her children by a previous marriage.[22]

The two boys in the company were also members of the Young family. Seven-year-old Isaac Perry Decker was a son of Harriett and a brother of Clara. Six-year-old Lorenzo Zobieski Young was the son of Lorenzo Young by another wife, Persis Goodall.

For three members of the company, the journey was a passport to freedom. Oscar Crosby, Hark Lay, and Green Flake were slaves. Oscar and Hark belonged to wealthy members of the Church in Mississippi. In October 1846, they set out for Winter Quarters, carrying a wagon load of supplies and instructions to assist the Saints on their journey westward. Two other members of the party died along the way. Green Flake was born on the plantation of his master, James Flake, and was brought to Nauvoo before the exodus. He was baptized in 1844 and was given to Brigham Young by James Flake.[23] Brigham Young doesn't mention Green Flake in his journal, and it is not certain what the status of any of the three slaves was during the migration from Winter Quarters.

As the time of departure for the mountains approached, one of the busiest persons in Winter Quarters was Father John Smith. This uncle of Joseph Smith had been a Patriarch since 1844, and in the ten years before his death in 1854, he pronounced 5,560 patriarchal blessings upon the heads of migrating Saints. At Winter Quarters, members were seeking blessings in the same manner they had sought temple endowments at Nauvoo. Father John's blessings, bound into seven large volumes, are still in the possession of the Church Historical Department, and copies are available to the descendants of those who received them.

One of them, dated March 23, 1847, was given to Margaret Cowan Bryson, the widow from County Down, Ireland, who had driven Mary Fielding's ox team from Nauvoo to Winter Quarters. As Margaret prepared for the earliest possible departure from Winter Quarters, she received this comforting blessing:

Winter Quarters, March 23, 1847. A blessing by John Smith, Patriarch, upon the head of Margaret Bryson, daughter of Samuel and Margaret Cowan, born County Down, Ireland, August, 1797.

Beloved sister, I place my hands upon thy head and seal upon thee a Father's blessing in the name of Jesus Christ. Inasmuch as thou hast left thy native land for the gospel's sake, the Lord is pleased, and thy name is written in the book of life, and he will add unto thee friends, houses, lands, riches, honors and every desirable blessing because of thy honesty and integrity of thy heart. No good thing shall be withheld from thee, for thou art of the blood of Ephraim, and a lawful heir to the Priesthood and all the blessings of Abraham, Isaac and Jacob that ever was conferred upon a female. Thy children shall be partakers of the new and everlasting covenant. Thou shalt have thy desire concerning them; they shall become a mighty people, and thou shalt never want friends to assist them to accomplish all they desire. Thy name shall be held in honorable remembrance in the house of Israel, and thy years shall be according to the desire of thy heart. Therefore, be patient, sister, and suffer not your faith to fail in times of trial, and not one [illegible] shall fail, and thou shalt be lifted up at the last day with thy Father's house. Amen.[24]

The promises have been kept gloriously. On June 17, less than two months after receiving her blessing, Margaret was on her way, driving her own ox team as one of 318 Saints in Abraham Smoot's company, which arrived in Salt Lake Valley, September 25, 1847.[25]

When the first body of pioneers left Winter Quarters on April 14, William Clayton, who had complained of one sickness after another during the winter, was suffering from rheumatism in his face; but at 11 A.M., Brigham Young and Dr. Willard Richards came to his home. He recorded: "Brigham told me to rise up and start with the pioneers in half an hour's notice." Within the half hour, he had packed up some needed supplies, had said good-bye to his family, and was on his way to the pioneer rendezvous, forty-seven miles west of Winter Quarters on the Elkhorn River. Two days later, he listed in his diary every one of the 148 members of the company, and as they went on their way he wrote: "there were 72 wagons, 93 horses, 52 mules, 66 oxen, 19 cows, and 17 dogs, and chickens." William Clayton's journal gave complete details as to how the company was organized, how the camps were guarded, and it contained valuable instructions that would benefit scores of other companies yet to come.

Orson Pratt was the scientist of the company. He was the surveyor, astronomer, and mathematician. William Clayton found him to be a source of daily interest. Orson carried with him a telescope so fine that William was able to observe all four of Jupiter's moons. The company was but four days on its way when the two men were walking together. William gave a suggestion to Orson. He had the idea of fixing a set of wooden cogwheels to the hub of a wagon wheel in order to tell the exact number of miles traveled each day. Orson Pratt approved, and the idea for what William Clayton later called the roadometer was born.

With its daily use, William Clayton began recording the distance of each day's travel and the distance from Winter Quarters. Upon his return to Winter Quarters, he was ready to make his valuable information available to thousands of travelers over the next two decades. Summarizing the successful trip, he wrote:

> We have been prosperous on our journey home, and have arrived in nine weeks and three days, including a week's delay waiting for the Twelve and killing buffalo. Our health has been remarkably good, but we have lacked provisions, many of us having nothing but dry buffalo meat. I have succeeded in measuring the whole distance from the City of the Great Salt Lake to this place, except a few miles between Horse Creek and the *A La Bonte* river, which was taken from the measurement going up. I find the distance to be 1,032 miles and am now prepared to make a complete travelers' guide from here to the Great Salt Lake, having been careful in taking the distance from creek to creek, over bluffs, mountains, etc. It has required much time and care and I have continually labored under disadvantages in consequence of the companies feeling no interest in it.
>
> The health of my family has encouraged me for all that is past, and my secret gratitude shall ascend to Heaven for the unbounded kindness and mercies which the Almighty has continually poured upon them in my absence.[26]

During the next year, William received so many requests for his travelers' guide, that he decided to publish it. It was printed in St. Louis in 1848 and would serve another generation of emigrants on their way across the plains.[27]

Except for those who had remained in the valley to plant crops and otherwise prepare for the oncoming thousands, the pioneer company was back in Winter Quarters on October 21, six months and one week after leaving for the mountains. They had spent three weeks in Salt Lake Valley, had located the temple site, and had dedicated the land as the gathering place of the Saints. At the completion of the journey, President Young called all the pioneers together for a farewell message. He said:

> Brethren, I will say to the Pioneers, I wish you to receive my thanks for your kindness and willingness to obey orders; I am satisfied with

you; you have done well. We have accomplished more than we expected. Out of one hundred forty three men who started, some of them sick, all of them are well; not a man has died; we have not lost a horse, mule or ox, but through carelessness. The blessings of the Lord have been with us. If the brethren are satisfied with me and the Twelve, please signify it. (which was unanimously done) I feel to bless you all in the name of the Lord God of Israel. You are dismissed to go to your homes.[28]

On the return trip, the pioneers had met five other companies totaling some 1,500 persons. All had left Winter Quarters on June 17. They followed the well-marked trail and arrived in Salt Lake Valley in September. The following May, Brigham Young would lead the largest of the emigrant companies, 1,200 Saints, into the valley.[29]

The question remains: How definitely had Brigham and his Council selected Salt Lake Valley as the final destination? Perhaps a satisfactory answer can be found in his journal dated July 23, the day before he proclaimed "This is the place."

> Friday, 23. The advance company moved about three miles and encamped. Elder Orson Pratt called the camp together, dedicated the land to the Lord, entreated the blessings on the seeds about to be planted and the labors of His saints in the valley. The camp was organized for work. Elders W. Richards and George A. Smith exhorted the brethren to diligence. . . .
>
> I ascended and crossed over the Big Mountain; when on its summit I directed Elder Woodruff, who had kindly tendered to me the use of his carriage, to turn the same half way round so that I could have a view of a portion of Salt Lake valley. The spirit of light rested over me and hovered over the valley, and I felt that there the Saints would find protection and safety.[30]

The rewards of the months at Winter Quarters were glorious, and happy Saints could see beyond their struggles to the careful planning, the fervent prayers, and the devotion to the Word and Will of the Lord that made the triumph possible.

Brigham Young, the President of the Quorum of the Twelve, had worn the mantle of leadership with dignity and devotion. On Sunday, December 5, the Quorum assembled at the home of Orson Hyde in Winter Quarters, to discuss affairs of the Church and plans for the next season's migration. Eight members of the Quorum were present and each spoke. Then, Brigham Young was unanimously elected President of The Church of Jesus Christ of Latter-day Saints.[31]

Three weeks later, a conference of the Church was held in the newly built tabernacle at Miller's Hollow, across the Missouri in Council Bluffs (newly named Kanesville). The new Presidency of the Church, Brigham Young, Heber C. Kimball, and Willard Richards were sustained unanimously. The evacuation of Winter Quarters had begun, but the site would continue to serve for another season. Later, in a surprising rebirth, it would serve for many more years in the epic history of Latter-day Saint migration.

Chapter Nine

SOME WHO STAYED

Today, the land on every side of the Winter Quarters site is a rich part of America's breadbasket. The Mormon pioneers marched right through this fertile country, forded the streams that annually brought silt to enrich its precious topsoil, and blazed their trail into an unknown wilderness. Understandably, there were some who stayed behind rather than venture into the unknown. The number of Mormons who decided not to join in the migration to Utah has not been determined, but there are evidences that there were many.

Elder Andrew Cunningham was called in 1855 to go to Florence, at the old Winter Quarters site, to assist with the annual emigration to the West. During his visit, he called upon some of the "old Mormons" in western Iowa. At a meeting in the old bowery in Salt Lake City, two years later, he told the Saints: "I found that it was not a very pleasant business, for there were almost all kinds of spirits among them except the true spirit of the gospel." He told of divided branches: half following one leader and the rest another. In Missouri and Illinois, he visited many "old Mormons," but found very few who had any disposition to come to the mountains. "Many of them" he said, "feel quite above those Saints that President Young led to Utah. They do not associate with those that left Illinois, neither do they associate with those that are favorable in emigration to this country."[1]

On April 12, 1860, Elder Jacob Gates, returning from a mission to England, wrote from Florence:

> Since I came to this place, I have been quite astonished to find so many people who once belonged to the Church of Jesus Christ of Latter-day Saints. Many of them are waking from a dream and are rubbing their eyes to ascertain if they can see. . . . I have been much gratified

to find that Elders Martindale and Wareham have gathered up the rem-
nants which have been left from England, Scotland, Wales, Denmark,
Sweden and almost every place under the whole heavens, and out of
these scattered fragments have organized several branches of the
Church, numbering several hundred souls, who are anxious to gather
to the valleys of Utah.[2]

There were many who did not hear or did not follow the preach-
ings of such eager missionaries. There were others who were
rounded up by various splinter groups that broke away from the
Church following the martyrdom of the Prophet Joseph Smith. At
least two such groups grew out of the Winter Quarters experience.
Their leaders had once been strong in the faith and had held posi-
tions of leadership in the Church.

One such was Alpheus Cutler, sixty-two years old when the
Saints came to Winter Quarters; he was known as Father Cutler
to many who knew and loved him.[3] Alpheus had been a member
of the Church since January 20, 1833, when he was baptized by
Elder David W. Patten. Born in New Hampshire, February 29, 1784,
Alpheus was a veteran of the War of 1812. Soon after the war, he
moved to New York state where the missionaries found and converted his entire family, then consisting of Alpheus, his wife Lois,
and eleven children. The event that brought the entire family into
the Church was the healing of a daughter, Lois, after an administration by Elder Patten. The family soon moved to Kirtland, Ohio,
to join the body of the three-year-old Church that Elder Patten
represented.[4]

He arrived in Kirtland at about the time of the groundbreaking
and cornerstone laying of the Kirtland Temple, and was one of the
workmen commended by the Prophet for the successful completion of that edifice. He was given a special blessing for his good
work.[5] This blessing gave him a lasting interest in temple building,
and when he joined the major exodus to Missouri, he was determined to build the House of the Lord in that state.

The Mormons had already been driven from Jackson and Clay
counties and had begun to build still another city at Far West, in
Caldwell County. On July 4, 1838, the Saints celebrated the birth
of the nation to which they pledged allegiance, still firm in the
belief that in this nation they could find protection for the practice
of their religion without persecution. A highlight of that ceremony
was the laying of four cornerstones for the Far West Temple, a

ceremony in which Alpheus Cutler played an important role. His
biographer states that on this occasion he was appointed and ordained by Joseph Smith to be the "chief architect and master work-
man of all God's holy houses."[6]

In a dramatic event less than a year later, Alpheus Cutler's
position was verified. A few days after the Independence Day ceremony, the Prophet Joseph Smith announced a revelation. Dated
July 8, 1838, it directed that the Quorum of the Twelve be fully
organized. It said: "Next spring, let them depart to go over the
great waters, and there promulgate my gospel, the fullness thereof
and bear record of my name. Let them take leave of my saints in
the city of Far West, on the twenty sixth day of April next, on the
building spot of my house, saith the Lord."[7]

On the day specified, most of the Saints had moved from Missouri to Quincy, Illinois, and the vicinity. Joseph Smith, recently
escaped from a long confinement in the Liberty Jail, had just made
his way to join them. Enemies of the Church had waved the
prophecy of July 8 in the faces of the Saints and swore it would
never be fulfilled. But on April 26 , six members of the Quorum
of the Twelve somehow made their way to Far West. They ordained
two new Apostles, Wilford Woodruff and George A. Smith, to fill
vacancies in the Quorum. Then the eight Apostles and a group of
assistants proceeded to the business at hand. The minutes of their
meeting read as follows:

> Elder Alpheus Cutler, the master workman of the house, then
> recommended laying the foundation of the Lord's house, agreeable to
> revelation, by rolling up a large stone near the southeast corner . . . .
> Elder Alpheus Cutler placed the stone before alluded to in its regular
> position, after which, in consequence of the peculiar situation of the
> Saints, he thought it wisdom to adjourn until some future time, when
> the Lord shall open the way, expressing his determination then to pro-
> ceed with the building; whereupon the conference adjourned. Thus was
> fulfilled a revelation of July 8, 1838, which our enemies had said could
> not be fulfilled, as no Mormon would be permitted to be in the state.[8]

When the Saints from Missouri found refuge in Nauvoo and
began building their city, Alpheus Cutler was still valiant in the
work of building a new temple. This, he had felt, was his special
assignment, but there were many more. In January 1841, the revelation ordering the building of the Nauvoo Temple also listed that
a high council be organized "for the cornerstone of Zion." Alpheus
Cutler was named one of its members.[9] He was always close to

the Prophet, and when Joseph and Hyrum were killed in Carthage Jail, he was one of the small body of men who secretly buried their bodies in the basement of the Nauvoo House.[10]

After the Prophet's death, Alpheus followed the leadership of Brigham Young and the Quorum of the Twelve; and when the Saints found it necessary to leave Nauvoo and begin their westward migration, Alpheus was listed as captain of one of the first twenty-five companies.[11] Although he was sixty-two years old, he withstood all the rigors of the trek across Iowa, camped with the Saints at Council Bluffs, and crossed with them to the west bank of the Missouri. There was founded what at first appeared to be a temporary city. It was named Cutler's Park by Brigham Young who recorded: "Elder Cutler having first selected the spot."[12]

The move from Cutler's Park was not in any sense an affront to Alpheus Cutler. There were good reasons for seeking a new site, and "Father Cutler" was named a member of the committee to locate Winter Quarters. When the new location was laid out and its streets platted, one of the principal streets was named "Cutler."[13]

That Alpheus Cutler was important in Brigham Young's organization for the governing of Winter Quarters is evident in a notation in President Young's diary for October 18, 1846. It read: "Prest. Alpheus Cutler called on the Bishops to guard their wards, seven of whom were present agreed to do so." Again, on November 3, a letter was written to Major Harvey, the Indian agent, concerning relations with the Indians and the prospects for the Saints to continue living on Indian lands west of the Missouri. The letter was signed "on behalf of the High Council of the Camp of Israel, Alpheus Cutler, President."[14]

In January of 1847, Brigham Young's revelation, "The Word and Will of the Lord, concerning the Camp of Israel in their journeyings to the West," was read to all the councils of the Church. Approval was unanimous, and there is no record of any objections by Alpheus Cutler. On January 26, captains were chosen for the various migrating companies, and Brigham Young's diary shows Alpheus Cutler as the president of Heber C. Kimball's company, with Winslow Farr and Daniel Russell as councilors.[15] Whether Alpheus Cutler's appointment was for the pioneer migration, or for a later period, is not made clear; but on March 13, as the departure date for the first pioneer company drew near, the Quorum of the Twelve met with a group of leading citizens to discuss the government and direction of affairs. Alpheus was among those consulted.

It is difficult to find, anywhere in available records, any friction or dispute between Brigham Young and Alpheus Cutler. But Alpheus never joined the migration to Utah, and when Brigham Young and other leaders returned to Winter Quarters in late 1847, Alpheus Cutler was ready to leave the Church. He took with him a number of other dissenters. After an unsuccessful attempt at fulfilling a mission to the Indians at Grasshopper, now Valley Falls, Kansas, Alpheus and his followers returned to southwestern Iowa, where they founded a community with the Book of Mormon name of Manti.[16]

It was there at Manti, on September 19, 1853, that Alpheus and those who had followed him joined together and proceeded to "re-organize the Church of Jesus Christ." Alpheus was named the "head, or Chief Counselor" of the new body. Edmund Fisher was named President, and Chancey Whiting was named Clerk of the Church. Clearly, despite the fact that another person held the title of President, Alpheus Cutler was the highest earthly authority recognized by the little group.[17] The Church of Jesus Christ (it never used the words *Latter-day Saints* in its title) still exists today and is commonly known as the Cutlerites. The church has divided into two groups, and a recent estimate of its membership is about forty-five in Independence, Missouri, and two or three families in Clitherall, Minnesota.

Alpheus Cutler died in 1864. He rendered distinguished service to The Church of Jesus Christ of Latter-day Saints over a period of more than twelve years. Why he left the Church is still not clear. The two Church doctrines that he challenged most, after breaking away, were plural marriage and the law of tithing. But records of eyewitnesses show he was present when the revelation on celestial marriage was read to the Nauvoo High Council in July of 1843. Two members of the Nauvoo Stake Presidency voted to reject it, but only one member of the High Council voted against it — and it was not Alpheus Cutler.[18]

The law of tithing was announced by the Prophet in Far West, Missouri, as a revelation from God on July 8, 1838. Alpheus Cutler was present and had participated on July 4 in laying the cornerstone for the Far West Temple. There is no record that he made any opposition to the law at that time, nor in the years that followed, either in Nauvoo or Winter Quarters.

Perhaps a more personal reason can be found for the break away. In February 1845, Clarissa Cutler, twenty-one-year-old daughter of Alpheus, became a plural wife of Heber C. Kimball. The following December, her seventeen-year-old sister, Emily, also was united in marriage to Heber. At the time of the exodus from Nauvoo in early 1846, both of the Cutler sisters were pregnant. Heber C. Kimball left them both in Nauvoo, and they came to Winter Quarters later. Clarissa's son, Abraham, was born in Nauvoo, April 16, 1846. Emily's son, Isaac, was born in Winter Quarters, October 13, 1846. When Heber left for the West with the pioneer company in April 1847, he took with him just one of his wives, Ellen Sanders Kimball. Left behind with their father were both Clarissa and Emily, with their sons.[19]

When the pioneers returned to Winter Quarters, with the plans of taking the rest of their families in the major migration of 1848, the Cutler sisters had evidently decided they could follow their husband no further. They separated from him in 1848 and accompanied their father to the settlements on Sugar Creek, Iowa, and then to the Indian mission in Kansas. There, in 1852, both of them died after having remarried. Their children, by both the first and second marriages, were taken into the home of the aging Alpheus Cutler.[20]

It is much easier to trace motives of another Mormon leader who chose to remain after the exodus from Winter Quarters. Like Alpheus Cutler, Bishop George Miller was deeply devoted to Joseph Smith. After an adventurous career throughout much of the western frontier, Bishop Miller found himself in Quincy, Illinois, in 1838. There he cleared some three hundred acres of land. He had reached Quincy just in time to hear of the "Mormon War" in Missouri, and he met some of its refugees. Two of them, Samuel H. Smith and Don Carlos Smith, brothers of the Prophet, became temporary tenants on George Miller's land. From them, he learned of the Prophet's escape from Missouri and vowed to see him. The opportunity soon came, as Bishop Miller later told in his memoirs:

> I perceived a carriage containing a number of persons meeting us; and as we neared it, the appearance of a large man, sitting in front, driving, seemed familiar to me as if I had always known him, and suddenly the thought burst into my mind that it was none other than the Prophet Joseph Smith. Indeed my whole frame was in a tremor at

the thought, and my heart seemed as if it were coming up into my mouth as he spoke:

"Sir, can you tell me the way to the farm of a Mr. Miller, living somewhere in the vicinity of the direction I am going?" . . .

"I presume, sir, that you are Joseph Smith, Jr., the Mormon prophet."

"I am, sir. I also presume that you are the Mr. Miller I inquired for."

With that spiritual introduction to the restored gospel, George Miller's conversion began. Soon another incident caused it to grow. Seriously ill and near death, he received a healing blessing at the hands of Sidney Rigdon and John Taylor. Bishop Miller wrote: "I was baptized by Elder Taylor, and a new era of my life was fully ushered in."[21]

He soon served a mission to Iowa, and shortly after his return, the Prophet had a new assignment for him. In a long revelation outlining much of the future of the Church, the word of the Lord was addressed to, among others, George Miller:

> And again, verily I say unto you, my servant George Miller is without guile; he may be trusted because of the integrity of his heart; and for the love which he has to my testimony I, the Lord, love him.
>
> I therefore say unto you, seal upon his head the office of a bishopric, like unto my servant Edward Partridge, that he may administer blessings upon the heads of the poor of my people, saith the Lord. Let no man despise my servant George, for he shall honor me.
>
> Let my servant George, and my servant Lyman, and my servant John Snider, and others, build a house unto my name, such a one as my servant Joseph shall show unto them, upon the place which he shall show to them also.[22]

For George Miller, it was a heady occasion and of great import to the future history of the Church. First, he was named the Presiding Bishop of the Church. He succeeded Edward Partridge, who had died in Nauvoo in 1840 from illnesses incurred during the Missouri persecutions. The second assignment given by revelation was even more portentous. He was assigned with Lyman Wight and others to build the Nauvoo House, which had been called in the revelation "A house for boarding, a house that strangers may come from afar to lodge therein."

From this assignment came the project to secure lumber from the Black River area of Wisconsin. Lyman Wight, George Miller, and a large company were to spend the next several years cutting the timber, preparing it, and shipping it to Nauvoo. It was at these

Wisconsin pineries that a plan grew to colonize Latter-day Saints in Texas. Whether or not this plan was a project of the Church is difficult to confirm. Bishop Miller's description, given in bitterness eleven years later, is worthy of note. He had returned to Nauvoo in the spring of 1844, and according to his letters in 1855, Joseph called a Council. Bishop Miller wrote:

> In this council it was agreed upon that we would run Joseph Smith for President of the United States, which we would certainly do, and also Sidney Rigdon for Vice President, and in case they were elected, we would at once establish dominion in the United States; and in view of a failure, we would send a minister to the then Republic of Texas, for all that country north of a west line from the falls of the Colorado River to the Nueces, then down the same to the Gulf of Mexico, and along the Rio Grande and up the same to United States territory, and get them to acknowledge us as a nation....
>
> Lucien Woodworth was chosen minister to Texas, and I was to return to the pineries to bring down Lyman Wight. We accordingly started the same day, Woodworth for Texas and I for the pineries....
>
> Some time toward the last of April, 1844, we (Lyman Wight, myself and families) arrived at Nauvoo. Soon after this, Woodworth returned from Texas. The Council convened to hear his report. It was altogether as we could wish it. On the part of the Church, there was commissioners appointed to meet the Texas Congress, to sanctify or ratify the said treaty, partly entered into by our minister and the Texas cabinet. A. W. Brown, Lucien Woodworth and myself were the Commissioners appointed to meet the Texas Congress, and upon the consummation of the treaty, Wight and myself were to locate the Black River Lumber Company on the newly acquired territory, and do such other things as might be necessary in the premises and report to the Council of the Kingdom.

In the meantime, there was the immediate business at hand, that of trying to get Joseph Smith elected as President of the United States. Bishop Miller was in Kentucky as an electioneerer when he learned of the martyrdom of Joseph and Hyrum Smith. He hurried back to Nauvoo and visited with John Taylor and Willard Richards, who had been in Carthage Jail with the Prophet when he was killed. According to Bishop Miller, he was told that there were sealed documents left, which would be opened when the Twelve Apostles should return. Then George Miller made a severe accusation. His words reveal the beginning of animosity toward the future leader of the Church, Brigham Young:

> Subsequent to these times of intense excitement, I had frequent attempts at conversation with Brigham Young and H. C. Kimball in regards to Joseph's leaving one to succeed him in the Prophet's office....

> I was invariably met with the inuendo "stop," or "hush brother Miller,
> let there not be anything said in regard to this matter, or we will have
> little Joseph killed as his father was," inferring directly that Joseph
> Smith had appointed his son Joseph to succeed him in the prophetic
> office.[23]

This was written in bitterness, years later. If he had heard such threats, it is hard to conceive why he would continue to follow Brigham Young's leadership. He was present on the occasion when Brigham Young and Sidney Rigdon contended before a public meeting of the Saints on the leadership of the bereaved Church. In view of many who were there, Brigham Young took on the appearance, voice, and mantle of Joseph Smith. It is strange to read George Miller's account of the same event. He recorded: "Young made a long and loud harangue, and as I had always took him to be a blunderbuss in speaking, and on this occasion to me apparently more so; for the life of me I could not see any point in the course of his remarks, than to overturn Sidney Rigdon's pretensions."

In Bishop Miller's narrative, the animosity continues. It is therefore surprising that on August 9, the day after the above incident, Brigham Young headed up a meeting of the seven members of the Quorum of the Twelve who were then in Nauvoo, and appointed Bishops Newel K. Whitney and George Miller as Trustees-in-Trust for the Church, succeeding Joseph Smith in this responsibility. On August 18, Brigham Young, in a Sunday sermon to the Saints, gave perhaps his first indication of friction between Bishop Miller and himself:

> There is no man who has any right to lead away one soul out of
> this city by consent of the Twelve, except Lyman Wight and George
> Miller; they have had the privilege of taking the Pine Company where
> they pleased, but not another soul has the consent of the Twelve to go
> with them. There is no man who has any liberty to lead away people
> into the wilderness from this church, or to lead them anywhere else,
> by the consent of the Twelve or the Church, except in the case above
> named—and I will tell you in the name of Jesus Christ that if Lyman
> Wight and George Miller take a course contrary to our counsel, and
> will not act in counsel with us, they will be damned and go to destruc-
> tion.[24]

It was already evident that Lyman Wight, a long respected member of the Quorum of the Twelve, was planning to go his own way, without the consent of other members of the Quorum. On August 24, 1844, the Quorum met with Lyman Wight present, and "he was counseled to go north, instead of going south."

Nevertheless, Lyman was clearly planning to leave for Texas. The following spring, with a group of his followers, principally from the Wisconsin pinery group, he was on his way. At the general conference of the Church in Nauvoo on April 6, 1846, Lyman Wight's status was considered and Brigham Young commented: "We should let him remain for the present. Probably hereafter there may be a time when he will hearken to counsel and do much good, which he is capable of—for he is a noble minded man." It was voted to continue his membership in the Quorum.

The conviction that Lyman Wight was "a noble minded man" continued with Brigham Young, long after Lyman Wight took a following of more than a hundred and established a colony in Texas. This took place in November 1845 before the Saints left Nauvoo. As late as October 1848, after Brigham Young had become President of the Church, he still led the Saints in sustaining Lyman Wight as a member of the Quorum of the Twelve. Reluctantly, he presided over his excommunication in February 1849.

Considering the animosity that George Miller felt toward Brigham Young, it seems strange that he did not accompany Lyman to Texas. Perhaps he felt deeply the obligation of being one of the two Presiding Bishops of the Church. Certainly, he was a leader in the movement westward. His wagons crossed the Mississippi February 6, 1846, among the first to begin the long struggle across Iowa.

He continued to separate himself from the leadership and move relentlessly on. On one occasion, Bishop Miller recalled: "The two brothers, O. and P. P. Pratt, and a company of others and myself had gone on ahead about eight miles, where we lay in camp a day or two, awaiting the coming up of Young, when a messenger arrived from Brigham with orders to return forthwith to their camps and give account of ourselves. We got on our horses and rode back. I remonstrated at their high handed measure. They said they had sent for us to have us in their council."[25]

Parley P. Pratt, writing of the same incident, recalled:

> We hastened on and met in Council. The President then reproved and chastened us severely for several things, among which was our drawing off from the council and main body of the camp and going ahead. He said there was manifest a spirit of dissension and insubordination in our movements. I could not realize this at the time, and protested that, in my own heart, as far as I was concerned, I had no

such motives, merely seeking to sustain the teams and people, and to make what progress we could, with that end in view.

However, the sequel soon proved that it was the true spirit which reproved and chastened us, for Bishop Miller, who was a leading and active member of our camp, has since left us and gone on his own way, having refused to be led by the Presidency, and removed to Texas. And here I will observe that, although my own motives were pure, as far as I could know in my own heart, yet I thank God for the timely chastisement. I profited by it, and it caused me to be more watchful and careful thereafter.[26]

For George Miller, it was but one more occasion for increasing his estrangement from Brigham Young and the Quorum. He continued to move ahead, crossed the Missouri far ahead of the leadership, and found a place for his own winter quarters. It was a site known as Running Water, among the Ponca Indians. It was some 150 miles west of the Winter Quarters selected by the Twelve. He followed counsel not to proceed farther west that season.

In January 1847, he was summoned to Winter Quarters for counsel with the leadership and was presented with Brigham Young's revelation, "The Word and Will of the Lord concerning the Camp of Israel in their journeyings to the West." In 1855, he wrote:

> When we got to Winter Quarters about the 28th of January, 1846 [1847], I had presented to me a revelation, given through Brigham Young, in regard to the journeyings of the saints west: Young indicated to me that a First Presidency would be organized.
>
> I was greatly disgusted at the bad composition and folly of this revelation, as also the intimation that a First Presidency would be organized, that I was from this time determined to go with him no longer.[27]

During this period, George Miller was doubtlessly in correspondence with Lyman Wight, who was firmly established in Texas. One of Bishop Miller's sons was a member of the Wight colony. In a broadside to all the Church in 1846, Lyman Wight wrote:

> We landed in Texas on the 16th of November, 1845, settling first at the falls above Austin, then in the valley of the Pedernales.
>
> These beautiful valleys in Texas . . . remind me of Ezekiel's vision of the tree of life, which has twelve manners of fruit and yielded its fruit every month, and the leaves were for the healing of the nations; for truly, in this country, we have the evergreen oak, the bay tree, muskeet and various other kinds of timbers, which you have never seen in the north. In fine, there are many kinds of vegetation that grow full better in the winter season than in the summer.
>
> I feel perfectly happy on my mission and thankful am I to God

that He ever put into the heart of Brother Joseph to assign me the
mission, that so many good and honest souls might be led from the
stern, inclement climate of the north, and from the low, sickly valleys
of the Mississippi River to a climate so congenial to the health, nature
and disposition of man.[28]

Bishop Miller's final break with Brigham Young came on April 3,
1847, as Brigham was preparing for the departure of the pioneer
company. President Young recorded in his journal: "Bishop George
Miller gave his views relative to the Church removing to Texas. . . .
I informed Bishop Miller that his views were wild and visionary,
that when we moved hence it would be to the Great Basin, where
the Saints would soon form a nucleus of strength and power sufficient to cope with mobs."[29]

Gathering with him a small group of followers, George Miller
began his exodus to Texas. He soon had a disagreement with Lyman
Wight, whom he described as having become a victim of alco-
holism. The disagreement was temporarily patched up, but George
Miller remained dissatisfied. Soon, he claimed to have received a
vision, which convinced him he should go to Michigan and join
James J. Strang, who had led a group of dissident Latter-day Saints
to form his own church on Beaver Island. Here, George Miller
spent the rest of his days.[30] He was dropped from his position as
Bishop before the departure for the West, and on October 20, 1848,
he was disfellowshipped from the Church.[31]

In addition to those who followed Alpheus Cutler and George
Miller away from Winter Quarters, there were others who chose
to remain on or near the banks of the Missouri. These scattered
into Iowa, Missouri, and Illinois, and with the departure of the
last wagons of the 1848 migration, Winter Quarters was deserted.[32]
There still remained, however, another glorious chapter in the
story, as the community consecrated in death and suffering was
resurrected and saw new life under a new name. Another decade
of glorious history was before it.

Chapter Ten

WINTER QUARTERS REBORN

Early in 1848, those members of the Church not yet ready to migrate to the Salt Lake Valley began the task of moving across the river into Iowa, to the Council Bluffs site that would soon be known as Kanesville. As the companies of Brigham Young, with 1,229 souls, and Heber C. Kimball, with 662, left the community that had been home for nearly two years, Brigham wrote: "Winter Quarters, after its vacation by Elder Kimball's company and mine, presented a desolate aspect. A terrific thunderstorm passed over, accompanied by a hurricane which tore wagon covers to shreds and whistled fearfully through the empty dwellings. A few straggling Indians camped in the vacated premises and subsisted on the cattle which had died by poverty, and what they could pick up."[1]

In October, Elder George A. Smith, one of those left in charge of the Iowa settlement, described the abandoned city. He wrote: "The Indians visited it of late and feasted on the potatoes that grew in the old cellars, also on the Indian corn and volunteer squash and such other vegetables as grew without culture. . . . Winter Quarters afforded more flies and fleas than anything less than a star-gazer could well estimate."[2]

It may seem a sad fate for what was once a prosperous city, but, after all, Winter Quarters was born to die. It had been just what its name implied, a winter quarters for the migrating Mormons. Now, the grassy mounds of the burying ground seemed the most enduring memento of the once thriving city.

But there would come a brighter day, after an interval of six years. In January 1854, Senator Stephen A. Douglas introduced a bill organizing Nebraska and Kansas as territories of the United States. This area beyond the Missouri, long considered Indian territory, now would be open to settlement. Senator Douglas's bill established the doctrine of popular sovereignty, and led to a land rush by proslavery and antislavery advocates that would become a violent prelude to the Civil War. The bustling ambitious city of Omaha came into being on the Missouri, a few miles south of old Winter Quarters. A newspaper, the *Omaha Arrow* was soon issued, and in its July 28, 1854, edition, it surveyed prospects for the area:

> Winter Quarters is also located up the river some ten miles above this city. It is pleasantly situated on a high bench and inclined plane, giving a fair and pretty view for a great distance around, and is the old site of the "Winter Quarters" of the Mormon Pioneers. The town is now being surveyed and improvements and public buildings erected. . . . A flat boat ferry is kept in operation for the benefit of settlers.

On September 9, proprietors of the Nebraska Winter Quarters claim held a meeting at the store of B. R. Pegram and Company, across the river in Council Bluffs. The proprietors drew plans to sell lots in the new community, which had been surveyed and given a new name—Florence, Nebraska. In a fashion still followed by real estate developers today, the new town was named for Florence Kilbourn, an adopted daughter of one of the organizers, James C. Mitchell.[3]

NEBRASKA

HISTORICAL MARKER

WINTER QUARTERS

Here in 1846 an oppressed people fleeing from a vengeful mob found a haven in the wilderness. Winter Quarters, established under the direction of the Mormon leader Brigham Young, sheltered more than 3,000 people during the winter of 1846-1847. Housed in log cabins, sod houses and dugouts, they lacked adequate provisions. When spring arrived more than six hundred of the faithful lay buried in the cemetery on the hill. Winter Quarters became the administration center of a great religious movement.

In the spring of 1847 a pioneer band left Winter Quarters to cross the Plains to the Great Salt Lake Valley. Thousands of others followed this trail. In 1855, Young was forced to utilize handcarts for transportation. The first company, comprising about five hundred persons, left here on July 17 and reached the Valley on September 26, 1856.

The town of Florence, established in 1854, was built upon the site of Winter Quarters. James C. Mitchell and Associates of the Florence Land Company established a thriving community. The Bank of Florence, built in 1856, stands today as a symbol of our historical past.

LDS Historical Church Archives

Historical marker explaining Winter Quarters and the founding of the city of Florence by James C. Mitchell

The new name was not approved everywhere. Later that year, a Mormon elder, Joseph E. Johnson, editor of the *Omaha Arrow,* wrote in his November 10, 1854, issue:

> We are decidedly "young Americans," yet we dislike these new fangled names which these reformers hitch on with a flourish to townsites, rivers, etc., throughout the territory. . . . Consider a pleasant townsite long and generally known as "Winter Quarters." . . . This grand old, significant and appropriate name has been changed to "Florence." Such new fangled fancy names don't suit us.

Soon the *New York Herald* had taken account of all the activity west of the Missouri. The paper's March 22, 1856, issue commented:

> The associations of this place, the old Mormon "Winter Quarters," as it is familiarly termed, are indeed quite pleasant. But about eight years ago, there were no less than 6,000 to 7,000 Mormons living here in comfortable houses, surrounded by well tilled farms. Indeed, Florence, or Winter Quarters, then presented the appearance of a thriving town, whilst it now bears scarce the resemblance of a settlement, but about a year ago there was, I think, two cabins upon the embryo town. The proprietors call it Florence; the good old "Winter Quarters" was not aristocratic enough.
>
> All the old Mormon houses have gone to decay or have burned down. The once thriving village of Latter-day Saints of 8 years ago has entirely passed away, rank weeds grow in plenteous confusion over the ruins, hiding the cellars and wells and all that remains of Winter Quarters.
>
> Just up yonder on that beautiful elevation was Brigham Young's house, whilst a little to the south you can see the outline of an old road. That road leads to the old Mormon burying ground, about one mile distant. There sleep hundreds of the Saints who forsook, for religious belief, comfortable houses in Europe to struggle here amid the toils and privation of frontier life and brace the inclemency of our severe winters. Side by side, they were buried here upon the prairie, and now a close observer can distinguish the little mounds stretched along the prairie over perhaps nearly a quarter of a mile.[4]

On November 4, 1854, at a meeting of the Nebraska Winter Quarters Company, a motion was made by A. Briggs, and was passed unanimously, that the President be authorized to purchase a half share in the company and tender it to Elder John Taylor, one of the Twelve Apostles of The Church of Jesus Christ of Latter-day Saints. Elder Taylor was at that time the Quorum member assigned to supervision of the migration to Salt Lake Valley. In 1855, the name of the developing company was changed to the Florence Land Company. Its records for April 7, 1856, show Elder Taylor acquired another twenty shares.[5]

Elder Taylor had an able assistant on the scene at Florence. On February 5, 1857, an advertisement appeared in the *Florence Courier*. It read:

EVERY VARIETY OF STAPLE AND FANCY DRY GOODS. FULL AND COMPLETE STOCK OF GROCERIES AND PROVISIONS, OILS, WINES AND PURE LIQUORS, WHICH FOR PRICE AND QUALITY CANNOT BE BEAT WEST OF ST. JOSEPH. LARGEST STOCK OF BOOTS AND SHOES IN THE TERRITORY OF NEBRASKA. READY MADE CLOTHING, NAILS, GLASS, HARDWARE, CUTLERY, IRON. HIGHEST PRICES WILL BE PAID FOR ALL KINDS OF COUNTRY PRODUCE. CASH PAID FOR DRY HIDES. OUR MOTTO IS: FAIR DEALING AND SMALL PROFITS.
ALEXANDER C. PYPER[6]

Alexander Cruickshanks Pyper was born in Largs, Ayrshire, Scotland, May 15, 1828. Missionaries of The Church of Jesus Christ of Latter-day Saints taught him the gospel, and at seventeen he became a traveling missionary for the Church in his native country. Arriving in the United States while the Saints were on their way westward, he settled for several years in St. Louis. In 1853, he moved to Kanesville, Iowa, and soon crossed the Missouri to open his mercantile business in the new town of Florence. There he married a nineteen-year-old New York girl named Christiana Dollinger, on Christmas eve, 1855. To this union would be born in Salt Lake City, in 1850, George Dollinger Pyper, famed manager of the Salt Lake Theatre and the Mormon Tabernacle Choir for many years.

In 1857, Horace S. Eldredge was called by the Church presidency for a second time to preside over the St. Louis conference of the Church and to act as emigration agent, under the direction of John Taylor. Horace Eldredge was quick to take advantage of Alexander Pyper's location and soon Latter-day Saints outfitting at Florence for their trip westward would find ready aid from the prospering Scotch merchant. In 1859, Alexander Pyper himself joined one of the companies formed at Florence and carried with him several wagon loads of merchandise to open a similar enterprise in Salt Lake City.[7]

Clearly, the establishment of the old Winter Quarters site as the outfitting point for the Mormon migration would be a financial benefit for the new community of Florence, and its proprietors hastened to take advantage of such a possibility. As early as September 13, 1854, the Nebraska Winter Quarters Company took its first steps to clean up and restore the old Mormon cemetery, left largely neglected after the departure of the last wagon trains of 1848.[8]

The first wagon train using Florence as its official outfitting point departed for the West on June 5, 1856, with Philemon C. Merrill as captain of 200 emigrants. Four more companies departed from Florence that season, bringing to 1,270 the total for the year. In addition 1,824 members of five handcart companies, formed at Iowa City, Iowa, that year, stopped to gather more supplies and commune with other Saints at the Florence outfitting headquarters.[9]

Elder Wandle L. Mace arrived with his family in Florence in 1856 to assist with the preparations there. A letter he wrote dated November of that year described the scene:

> A short distance north was a creek which emptied into the river. Across this creek rose a hill upon which the emigrating Saints camped on their route to the valley. On the highest point a warehouse was built, where goods of various kinds were deposited until they could be freighted to Utah. For a while, meetings were held in this building, until a dwelling was completed and occupied by a family named Kinney, which was home for the elders, who had charge of Church business; the upper room was used for meetings. . . .
>
> This was the last outfitting point before crossing the plains, and quite a business place during the summer while the Saints were preparing for their journey. The camping ground was the attraction, with its streets of tents, wagons and handcarts. . . .
>
> It was a peculiar sight, these companies of handcarts, with their little white covers, drawn by men and women as they passed through the town and over the western hills on their wearisome journey. A number of wagons, carrying tents and baggage which could not be carried in handcarts attended each company, also to assist the sick and lame should any become so. All seemed remarkably happy as they started on their long journey, and many were the prayers offered up that they might have success.
>
> In late October, a company of elders arrived in Florence from Salt Lake City, Parley P. Pratt among them. We had not met since the exodus from Nauvoo. He was intending to publish his autobiography. He had some corrections to make and some items to note of things that took place in New York City, some in my home. He spent most of the short time, two or three days he was in Florence, in my home. When we parted, it was with the expectation of meeting again the next summer—but I never saw him again.[10]

Parley P. Pratt was murdered in Arkansas the following May 11.

Florence was a welcome sight to the first two of the handcart companies. They had left Iowa City June 9 and 11 and arrived in Florence July 8, traveling approximately the same distance as the pioneer companies from Nauvoo to Winter Quarters a decade earlier. That journey had taken all spring and most of the summer. The handcarts made it in less than a month. Their arrival at Florence was described in a letter from J. H. Latey, written on August 14, 1856, and published soon after in the British Mission newspaper, *Millennial Star*. The letter read:

> The first and second companies of emigrants by handcarts, under the care of Captains Edmund Ellsworth and Daniel D. McArthur . . . arrived in camp on the 17th of July in fine health and spirits, singing as they came along Elder J. D. T. McAllister's noted handcart song, "Some must push and some must pull" etc. One would not think that they had come from Iowa City, a long and rough journey of from 275 to 300 miles, except by their dust-stained garments and sunburned faces. My heart is gladdened as I write this, for methinks I see their merry countenances and buoyant step, and the strains of the handcart song seem ringing in my ears like sweet music heard at eventide or in a dream.
>
> The first company had among its numbers the Birmingham band, and though but young performers, they played really very well, far superior to anything to be found this far west. In giving you the feelings of the first two companies, I give you in effect the feelings of the whole. This is the bright side of the picture, and is of those who may really be called Latter-day Saints; who have in continual remembrance the covenants they have made; who obey counsel and may really be called Saints of the Most High God.
>
> There are others—for I have seen both sides of the picture—who are apt to forget the God who has delivered them from their gentile chains and taskmasters, and are allured by fine promises and high wages; others there are whose faith is not of that nature to stand the trials they are called upon to undergo, and back out from five to fifty in a company of 300; but the mirth of the one kind does not interfere with the gloom of the other, or vice-versa, each does what suits him best.[11]

The account in the *Millennial Star* must have been welcome news to thousands of Saints in Great Britain. Most of the members of those first two handcart companies had sailed from Liverpool on March 23 aboard the *Enoch Train*. During the thirty-nine day voyage to Boston, four children were born. In high spirits, the parents named two of the children after the vessel that carried them to Zion. They were named Christina Enoch Lyon and Enoch Train Hargraves.[12]

In mid-August, Florence was a frantically busy place. On August 11, the fourth handcart company, headed by James G. Willie, arrived. It was already late in the season, and the company, consisting of Scotch, English, and Scandinavian Saints, had rushed to complete their handcarts at Iowa City and made their journey in twenty-eight days. The *Thornton*, which carried most of these emigrants, did not arrive in Boston until June 14, after forty-one days at sea.[13] Then came the long rail voyage to the Rock Island terminal at Iowa City. It was July 15 before the handcarts started rolling from Iowa City toward Florence.

There, far too many of the hastily built handcarts needed repairs. Some of them had to have new axles, and nearly all of them had to have pieces of iron attached to keep the wheel from wearing away the wood. This preparation took a full week, and it was August 18 before the string of handcarts, accompanied by supporting wagons to carry provisions, started westward again. There were some who feared that the company was starting too late in the season, and at Florence, an urgent meeting was held to discuss the subject. The call to come to Zion was too great to be silenced, and with only one dissenting vote, the leaders of the company decided to go forward. Levi Savage, who cast the dissenting vote, explained his reasons and then said: "Brethren and sisters, what I have said I know to be true, but seeing you are to go forward, I will go with you, will help you all I can, will work with you, will rest with you, will suffer with you and if necessary I will die with you. May God in his mercy bless and preserve us."

The Willie handcart company was barely out of Florence when another, under the leadership of Edward Martin, arrived. This company, too, hurried to repair its handcarts, replenish supplies, and continue onward. The fate of these two companies is well-known. Caught in the early storms of impending winter, they were delayed, ran out of provisions, and were rescued by forces sent from Salt Lake City. There were 67 deaths among the 500 members of the Willie company, and from 135 to 150 deaths of the 576 members of the Martin company.[14]

The fate of these two companies was tragic, but by no means a supreme tragedy. It was rather a demonstration that courageous men and women would undertake the greatest of trials to support their faith in God and trust in their leadership. At the year's end, the Church could survey the results of the first year's emigration by handcart. Out of 1,824 travelers, nearly 1,600 had reached their new homes in the valleys of Zion. A year-end epistle from the First Presidency summarized the year's activity:

> This season's operations have demonstrated that the Saints, being
> filled with faith and the Holy Ghost, can walk across the plains, drawing

their provisions and clothing in handcarts. . . . The entire trip from Iowa City, a distance of over 1,300 miles to this city, has been accomplished in less traveling days than it has ever been by ox train or wagon and with far greater ease to the travelers. These companies, with the exception of the last two, which started too late in the season, have made the trip from the Missouri River in a little over two months.[15]

Heading up the recommendations for the next season was the firm edict that "no company must be permitted to leave the Missouri River later than the 1st day of July." More and more, the Missouri River and Florence would be the central core of all the emigration plans. At the beginning of the 1856 season, William H. Kimball had been appointed by Elder John Taylor to go to the old Winter Quarters site and make arrangements for the Church's operations there. On April 4, he wrote to Elder Taylor in New York and said:

> I arrived here yesterday and have had an interview with the proprietors of the town, with whom I have completed arrangements for making this the permanent starting point and outfitting place for our emigration. . . .
> The destiny of Florence is onward and upward. . . . I feel confident that the time is not far distant when Florence will be recognized as the great commercial center, not only of Nebraska but of the upper Missouri generally.[16]

William Kimball had evidently accepted much of the heavy propaganda dispensed by the Florence Land Company as it struggled with Omaha to become the queen city of the Upper Missouri; but there was no doubt of the importance of Florence in the Church's emigration plans. As the 1857 season approached, there came a dramatic demonstration of handcart travel, which had come to some disfavor through the tragedy of the Willie and Martin companies. On June 10, 1857, there came whooping into Florence from the West a jubilant handcart company. They consisted of seventy missionaries who had traveled from Salt Lake City in the unbelievable time of 40½ days. Unencumbered by any slow moving wagons, these missionaries had carried all their food and supplies in the handcarts.

The *Florence Courier* found their arrival the biggest news of the week, and its reporter went into the handcart camp for details. His report read:

> The bodies of the carts were tastefully painted and with such inscriptions on the sides as "Truth Will Prevail," "Zion's Express,"

"Blessings Follow Sacrifice" and "Merry Mormons.". . . From the accounts published in the various journals throughout the country, the general impression on the mind of the public is that the handcart is the slowest and most laborious mode of conveyance that can be used. From the report of this party and of others, we are inclined to think exactly the reverse. This party was but nineteen days in coming from Fort Laramie, a distance of 520 miles — an average of over 27 miles a day — some days they made 35 miles. . . . The members of the party were Elders going on missions to different parts of the world. They were feeling fine after their trip and expressed themselves to be on hand for a foot race or wrestling match with any one in Florence who might be inclined to indulge. The party sold their wagons at prices ranging from eight to twelve dollars. They cost forty dollars to build in the valley.[17]

On June 13, the first westbound handcart company of the new season, headed by Elder Israel Evans, rolled into town. After a week's final preparation, it was on its way westward. A second handcart company and four wagon companies would leave Florence that season, bringing the number of emigrants through the Missouri port to 1,214. On the day the first handcart company reached Florence, the first wagon train was ready to depart. Under the leadership of William Walker, it was made up of Saints already assembled at Florence awaiting transportation. By wagon or handcart, Florence would soon be the official departure point for all Mormon migration.

In July 1857, Elder John Taylor paid a visit to Florence, a memorable return to the Winter Quarters he had left ten years earlier. He wrote of the experience:

Very great improvements have been made in the country on the border of the Missouri. Florence, however, is one of the prettiest sights I have ever seen. They have made rapid improvements here, and what was a few years ago a solitary place is now a thriving and rapidly increasing little city. . . .

In passing through this country, I am reminded forcibly of the time when we first traversed this land, and especially our sojourn at Winter Quarters. I visited the graves of many of our dead, and could not but reflect on the trying scenes we had passed through.

I felt like saying "sleep on, oh ye martyrs of truth, you are now at rest and all is well. No slanderer's tongue can longer bite as a viper; you are beyond the reach of mobs and mob violence."

Elder Taylor copied some of the names still legible from the Winter Quarters period. Among them were Joseph Smith Turley and Hyrum Smith Turley, twin sons of Theodore Turley. He had been a fellow Methodist preacher with Elder Taylor in Toronto before they heeded the gospel message of Parley P. Pratt.[18]

In February 1857, there appeared at the door of Elder Wandle Mace, in Florence, an old man carrying a satchel and appearing to be very sick. Elder Mace welcomed him and invited him to sit down. The man then introduced himself as Thomas B. Marsh, once a member of the Quorum of the Twelve Apostles. He was one of the original members of that Quorum and soon became its president. Two revelations of the Doctrine and Covenants were specifically addressed to him. Had he maintained his position in the Quorum, he, instead of Brigham Young, might have been leading the Church. But on that cold February day of 1857, sick and looking much older than his fifty-seven years, he presented to Wandle Mace a pathetic image.

In a conference address in April 1984, President Gordon B. Hinckley, then Second Counselor in the First Presidency, told of the circumstances that changed the life of Thomas B. Marsh. It began with a simple quarrel between Thomas Marsh's wife and a Sister Harris, in Far West, Missouri, in 1838. The quarrel was over the use of "strippings" from the cows milked by the two neighbors. Thomas Marsh defended his wife's position before his bishop, and a Church trial was held. When the decision went against Sister Marsh, her husband appealed to the High Council and then to the Presidency of the Church. There, too, the decision was against him, and Thomas B. Marsh began a period of rebellion against the Church. He was soon relieved of his Presidency of the Quorum, and on March 17, 1839, he was excommunicated for apostasy.[19]

Nineteen years later, humble, dejected, and old before his time, he sat in the home of Wandle Mace in Florence, Nebraska, and asked to be rebaptized into the Church. Because of the high position he had once held, Elder Mace felt he should appeal to higher authority. Thomas Marsh understood and waited at Florence for the first wagon train of the season to carry him to Salt Lake City. On June 13, he joined the company of Captain William Walker. Somewhere between Florence and Salt Lake City, Apostles John Taylor and Erastus Snow caught up with the Walker company, and at the first available water, Thomas B. Marsh was rebaptized.[20]

In September, at a sacrament meeting held in the old bowery in Salt Lake City, Brigham Young welcomed him back into the fold. Brother Marsh told the congregation: "My voice was never very strong, but it has been very much weakened of late by the afflicting rod of Jehovah. He loved me too much to let me go without whipping. I have seen the hand of the Lord in the chastisement which I have received." Nine years later, in Utah, he died a faithful member of the Church.

The year 1857 brought another event of great portent to the future of Florence. Before the opening of the emigration season, a new Missouri River steamboat named the *Florence* was launched. It would be one of many steamboats operating up and down the Missouri. The railroad had reached St. Louis and would soon be into St. Joseph. Emigrants could take the train all the way to these Missouri ports and then the steamboat to Florence.[21]

But 1857 was also a year of troubles. At the Pioneer Day celebration on July 24, the Saints learned that an invading army of the United States was on its way to the Territory of Utah to put down what was called a rebellion of the people against government authority. Meanwhile, a nationwide panic was having its effect on banking and commercial interests in Florence. The combined effect

The old Bank of Florence, established in 1856

LDS Historical Church Archives

would slow down emigration. There were but three relatively small wagon companies who left Florence for the West in 1858.

In 1859, things were better. One handcart company and four wagon companies, all organized at Florence, carried 1,431 Saints to Utah. Each company made the journey in less than three months. The thorough preparations at the staging point were proving eminently successful.

The last of the handcart companies, numbers nine and ten, opened the busy 1860 season. They were followed by eight wagon companies, bringing the total number of emigrants from Florence that year to 2,091.[22] The event that brought an end to handcart travel was noted in Florence on July 1. A company of missionaries bound for Europe arrived on that day, only sixty-five days out of Salt Lake City. The trip was an experiment, using a new generation of mountain oxen. Its success demonstrated the fact that mountain cattle could withstand the round-trip, crossing the plains twice in one season, better than cattle, horses, or mules purchased by the Church in the midwest.[23]

In the October 1860 general conference, Brigham Young praised highly the success of the ten handcart companies, but believed the Church had found a better way. He said:

> If we can go with our teams to the Missouri River and back in one season, and bring the poor, their provisions, etc., it will save about half the cash we now expend bringing the Saints to this point from Europe. It now costs in cash nearly as much for their teams, wagons, handcarts, cooking utensils, provisions, etc. for their journey across the plains as it does to transport them to the frontiers. We can raise cattle without an outlay of money and use them in transporting the Saints from the frontiers. . . .
>
> Brethren and sisters, save your fives, tens, fifties, a hundred dollars, or as much as you can until next spring; and send your money, your cattle and wagons to the States, and buy your goods and freight with them. Twenty dollars expended in this way will do as much good as several times that amount paid to the stores here.[24]

The gathering clouds that resulted in the Civil War were growing thicker as President Young made his Conference address. Before the first emigrating company left Florence the following year, the bitter fighting was under way. When it began, three sailing ships were already on the high seas, bringing more than 2,500 Saints to Zion. To the Presidency, the plan of sending teams from Salt Lake City to Florence became supreme urgency. No longer a mere matter of money-saving convenience, it was a rescue mission. Besides those overseas, there were hundreds of others waiting at Florence and many other places to join the first emigrant teams of the season. The words "Israel, Israel, God is calling, calling thee from lands of woe" never seemed more urgent, and a call for assistance went out through the valleys of the mountains.

The Church epistle sent out that spring not only called for personal sacrifice to help distressed brothers and sisters, it pointed out numerous advantages to the people of Utah. It would provide a ready market for their cattle. The teamsters could not only bring four oxen for each wagon, but also additional cattle that could serve as oxen for companies being made up in Florence in addition to the rescuers. Flour and meat could be deposited at various way stations along the way and picked up by oncoming emigrant trains. In addition, many other Utah products that might be loaded in the wagons could find ready sale in the crowded city of Florence.

The response to the appeal of the First Presidency was overwhelming. From the Salt Lake Valley, forty-eight wagons with their teamsters were volunteered. Others came from every part of the state. They came from Beaver, Cedar City, and Parowan in the far south and from fourteen communities in Utah County. Twenty-six teams came from the far north: Logan, Smithfield, Wellsville, Willard, and Boxelder, and also Franklin, Idaho. They also came from Tooele and Grantsville to the west and from Weber and Davis counties. All in all, 185 teamsters with wagons and oxen answered the call.[25]

Twelve large wagon companies made 1861 one of the great years of Mormon emigration. They carried 3,451 Saints. The largest company, made up of 620, was headed by Milo Andrus. His company had been under his leadership all the way from Liverpool, where he had completed his mission and was placed in charge of the large number of English converts aboard the *Underwriter*. It arrived in New York on May 22; the company traveled by rail and river to Florence and was ready to roll in good wagons, pulled by sturdy mountain oxen.

Another missionary returning from Britain was Homer Duncan, assigned to the leadership of his company. So successful was his trip that he accepted a call to drive to Florence the following year and bring another five hundred Saints to Zion. Joseph Horne was called from a pioneering cotton farm on the Virgin River in Southern Utah. He, too, would lead a group of volunteers to Florence and back the next season. Sixtus Johnson was called for a round trip from the same remote Virgin River area. John R. Murdock was a sturdy pioneer of plains travel. He had been a member of the Mormon Battalion and of the rescuers sent to save the stranded Willie and Martin handcart companies. In Utah, he was one of the earliest settlers of Lehi, and from there he was called in 1861 to make the round-trip to Florence. In the next seven years, he would make five such trips across the plains.[26]

There were thirteen wagon companies that departed from Florence in 1862 and twelve in 1863. But while the Church emigration work was prospering, the general prosperity of Florence was floundering. The Bank of Florence never recovered from the panic of 1857 and closed its doors in 1859. James C. Mitchell, the most active of Florence promoters, died shortly thereafter, and the deciding blow to the community's future came when the oncoming railroads chose Omaha rather than Florence as its crossing point.[27]

The decline of Florence and the move of railroad activity further south were among the reasons for changing the staging area for Church emigration from Florence to Wyoming, Nebraska, forty miles down the Missouri near Nebraska City. Florence, however, did not decay and disappear. As Omaha grew, it became an important suburb and finally an annexed part of the fast-growing city.

Florence has preserved its identity and its memories of the days when it was a prime starting point for the greatest migration in American history. In the years 1847 to 1862, there departed from Winter Quarters and its successor, Florence, forty-seven wagon companies and ten handcart companies, carrying more than fourteen thousand Saints to their new homes in the mountains. In addition, there were the hundreds who began their journey farther eastward and made Florence their final post for replenishing their stocks and refurbishing their equipment.

St. Louis has its mighty Gateway Arch to herald it as the "gateway to the West." Independence celebrates its place as the beginning of the Santa Fe Trail. The Winter Quarters story needs to be recognized too. Its contributions were many, and its rich history and even richer results should never be forgotten.

APPENDIX

This is a list of the deaths and burials in the Camp of Israel at Cutler's Park and Winter Quarters, 1846-48. It was compiled by Ethel B. Kirby from early Church records loaned to the Genealogical Society of Utah by the Church Historian's office.

Adams, Henry (46 yrs.)
> Son of Henry and Jennah Adams
> Died: Nov. 10, 1846, of dysentery
> Born: Jan. 7, 1800, Barnstead, Lower Canada

Aikens, Samuel F. (20 yrs.)
> No survivors listed
> Died: Feb. 27, 1847, of canker
> Born: Jan. 7, 1827, New Salem, Franklin County, Mass.

Akley, John (34 yrs.)
> Husband of Jane Akley
> Died: Oct. 24, 1846
> Born: Dec. 24, 1811, N.Y.

Alexander, Nancy (29 yrs.)
> Wife of Horace B. Alexander
> Died: Jan. 28, 1847
> Born: Dec. 8, 1817, Dayton, Ohio

Allen, Joseph D. (5 mos.)
> Son of Joseph S. and Lucy D. Allen
> Died: Aug. 17, 1847, of chills and canker
> Born: Feb. 25, 1847, rush bottoms above Winter Quarters

Alsworth, Orson H. (1 yr.)
> Son of David and Catherine Alsworth
> Died: Nov. 12, 1846, of canker
> Born: Nov. 7, 1845, Lee, Lee County, Iowa

Anderson, Adney A. C. (5 mos.)
> Son of Buckley B. and Sally M. Anderson
> Died: May 11, 1847, of inflammation of the bowels
> Born: Dec. 9, 1846, Winter Quarters

Angell, Almira (3 days)
Daughter of Truman O. and Polly Angell
Died: Nov. 1, 1846, at Cutler's Park
Born: Oct. 29, 1846, Cutler's Park

Angell, Marthy Ann (10 yrs.)
Daughter of Truman O. and Polly Angell
Died: Dec. 2, 1846, of fever
Born: July 6, 1836, Gage County, Ohio

Angell, Truman C. (2 yrs.)
Son of Truman O. and Polly Angell
Died: Sept. 30, 1847, of measles
Born: Jan. 20, 1845, Nauvoo, Ill.

Angus, William (74 yrs.)
Husband of Agnes G. Angus
Died: Oct. 26, 1846
Born: Apr. 1771, Sterling Co., Scotland

Armstrong, Mary (48 yrs.)
Daughter of James and Elizabeth Gibbons
Died: Aug. 21, 1847, of chills and fever
Born: 1799, Tennessee

Arnold, Caroline (12 yrs.)
Daughter of Josiah and Elizabeth Arnold
Died: Sept. 30, 1847, of canker
Born: 1845, Oswego County, N.Y.

Arrowsmith, Anna (age not listed)
Died: Nov. 2, 1846
Born: Augusta, Lee County, Iowa

Babcock, Amos (37 yrs.)
Husband of Mary Ann Babock
Died: Nov. 14, 1846, of consumption
Born: Aug. 5, 1809, Fortkin, Washington County, N.Y.

Babcock, Benjamin A. (11 yrs.)
Son of Amos and Mary Ann Babcock
Died: Mar. 17, 1847, of scurvy
Born: July 3, 1835, Fort Ann, Washington County, N.Y.

Babcock, Cirilla Jane (1 yr.)
Daughter of Amos and Mary Ann Babcock
Died: Feb. 4, 1847, of chills
Born: Jan. 7, 1847, Nauvoo, Ill.

Babcock, George (1 yr.)
Son of Lorenzo and Anna Babcock
Died: Aug. 9, 1847, of canker
Born: Feb. 27, 1846, Nauvoo, Ill.

Bailey, Elijah (1 yr.)
Son of Jerrey C. and Sarah Bailey
Died: Jan. 30, 1847, of concussion of the brain
Born: June 6, 1846, Mount Pisgah, Iowa

Baker, Susannah E. (17 yrs.)
Daughter of Benjamin and Abigail Baker
Died: May 7, 1848
Born: Dec. 26, 1830, Albion, N.Y.

Barton, Mary (74 yrs.)
Daughter of John and Abigail Cooley
Died: Oct. 22, 1847, of consumption
Born: Oct. 4, 1773, Huntington County, N.J.

Beakley, Mary (18 yrs.)
Daughter of John and Mary Beakley
Died: Dec. 7, 1846, of chills and fever
Born: Mar. 31, 1828, Chester County, Pa.

Bembo, Jane (54 yrs.)
Wife of John Bembo
Died: Nov. 28, 1846, of chills and fever
Born: Jan. 12, 1792, Ashburton, Herefordshire, England

Bigler, Susannah (61 yrs.)
Wife of Mark Bigler
Died: Mar. 14, 1847, of consumption
Born: Oct. 11, 1786, Charles County, Md.

Bilington, Sarah (37 yrs.)
Wife of Joshua Bilington
Died: Sept. 20, 1847, of canker
Born: 1810, England

Blackhurst, Margaret (43 yrs.)
No survivors listed
Died: Jan. 5, 1847, of canker
Born: May 1804, Longton, Lancastershire, England

Boggs, Francis (1 yr.)
Son of Francis and Evelina Boggs
Died: Jan. 23, 1847
Born: Oct. 23, 1845, Nauvoo, Ill.

Bosley, Edward (70 yrs.)
Husband of Ann Bosley
Died: Dec. 15, 1846, of shortness of breath
Born: June 25, 1776, Pennsylvania

Boss, Elizabeth S. (19 yrs.)
Wife of Alexander Boss
Died: Dec. 1, 1846, of chills and fever
Born: Apr. 6, 1827, Andover, Windsor County, Vermont

Bostwek, Leah (75 yrs.)
Daughter of Abraham and Alley Van Dason
Died: Dec. 1, 1846, of consumption
Born: Feb. 8, 1775, Dutchess County, N.Y.

Brewett, Moroni (1 yr.)
Son of Daniel and Eliza Brewett
Died: Dec. 26, 1846, of canker
Born: Sept. 8, 1845, Nauvoo, Ill.

Bringhurst, Charles H. (8 mos.)
Son of William and Ann Bringhurst
Died: Dec. 23, 1846
Born: Apr. 23, 1846, Nauvoo, Ill.

Brinkerhoff, James (1 yr.)
Son of James and Sally Ann Brinkerhoff
Died: Nov. 16, 1846, of canker
Born: Aug. 24, 1845, Nauvoo, Ill.

Brinton, Elizabeth H. (29 yrs.)
Wife of David Brinton
Died: Sept. 24, 1846, of chills and fever
Born: Sept. 17, 1817

Brinton, Robert H. (11 mos.)
Son of David and Elizabeth Brinton
Died: Oct. 17, 1846, of chills and fever
Born: Nov. 11, 1845, Nauvoo, Ill.

Brown, Emley Jane (6 days)
Daughter of Isaac and Hannah Brown
Died: May 26, 1847
Born: May 18, 1847, Winter Quarters

Bruce, Maryanne (36 yrs.)
Daughter of Jeduthem and Polly Simonds
Died: Oct. 8, 1846
Born: Apr. 27, 1810, Ishua, Allegheny County, N.Y.

Bullock, Isabella (2 yrs.)
No survivors listed
Died: Apr. 15, 1847, of scurvy
Born: July 7, 1844, Nauvoo, Ill.

Bullock, Janet (7 yrs.)
Daughter of James and Mary Bullock
Died: Feb. 18, 1847, of canker
Born: Dec. 23, 1839, Esso, Lime County, Upper Canada

Bullock, Willard Richards (2 yrs.)
Son of Thomas and Henrietta Bullock
Died: Mar. 17, 1847, of effects of persecution
Born: Feb. 11, 1845, Nauvoo, Ill.

Burdick, Ephraim (9 mos.)
  Son of Thomas and Anna Burdick
  Died: July 31, 1847, of summer complaint
  Born: Oct. 6, 1846, Montrose, Iowa

Burnham, Mary C. (19 yrs.)
  Wife of Jacob D. Burnham
  Died: Mar. 27, 1847, of scurvy
  Born: Feb. 20, 1828, Winsor, Hartford County, Conn.

Burnham, Mary Lowery (8 mos.)
  Daughter of Jacob and Mary C. Burnham
  Died: July 31, 1847, of summer complaint
  Born: Nov. 27, 1846, Winter Quarters

Busenbark, William J. (1 yr.)
  Son of Isaac and Abigail Busenbark
  Died: Feb. 8, 1848, of inflammation
  Born: Dec. 25, 1846, Winter Quarters

Butterfield, Percis (1 yr.)
  Daughter of Abel and Caroline Butterfield
  Died: Aug. 27, 1847
  Born: No information given

Butterworth, Sarah
  Died: Dec. 12, 1846, Winter Quarters
  Born: No information given

Caleyham, Lyman (1 yr.)
  Died: Oct. 27, 1846
  Born: Jan. 30, 1845, Nauvoo, Ill.

Calkins, Lumen Israel (1 yr.)
  Son of Lumen and Mahetable Calkins
  Died: July 22, 1847, of consumption
  Born: July 21, 1846, Council Bluffs, Iowa

Callister, Thomas (7 mos.)
  Son of Thomas and Caroline Callister
  Died: May 8, 1847
  Born: Sept. 13, 1846, Cutler's Park

Calvet, David (16 yrs.)
  No survivors listed
  Died: Feb. 10, 1847
  Born: Mississippi

Campbell, Charity (age unknown)
  Wife of Nathaniel Campbell
  Died: Jan. 24, 1847
  Born: No information given

Canfield, Myron C. (1 yr.)
Son of Cyrus and Clarissa Canfield
Died: Aug. 24, 1847, of canker
Born: Oct. 4, 1845, City of Joseph

Carpenter, Abigail (6 yrs.)
Daughter of Samuel Carpenter
Died: Sept. 22, 1846, of chills and fever
Born: Sept. 20, 1840, Macedony, Ill.

Carpenter, Samuel E. (43 yrs.)
Died: Sept. 25, 1846, of chills and fever
Born: Mar. 10, 1803

Carrington, Albert, Jr. (1 yr.)
Son of Albert and Rhoda M. Carrington
Died: Feb. 3, 1847, of scarlet fever
Born: July 23, 1845, Nauvoo, Ill.

Carter, Sally S. (21 yrs.)
Wife of Daniel Carter
Died: Feb. 10, 1847, of canker
Born: Sept. 1, 1826, Essex County, N.Y.

Cavet, Julia (age not given)
Orphan
Died: Mar. 5, 1848, of worms

Chamberlain, Hoopee (63 yrs.)
Wife of Solomon Chamberlain
Died: Jan. 12, 1847, of consumption
Born: 1778, Middleborough, Mass.

Clark, David W. (21 days)
Son of David P. and Sarah E. Clark
Died: Nov. 9, 1846
Born: Oct. 19, 1846, Winter Quarters

Clark, Felina (1 yr.)
Daughter of Lorenzo and Beulah Ann Clark
Died: Oct. 1, 1846, of fits
Born: Feb. 28, 1845, Nauvoo, Ill.

Clark, Gardner (56 yrs.)
Husband of Delecta Clark
Died: Apr. 11, 1847, of scurvy
Born: Jan. 15, 1791, Lee, Berkshire County, Mass.

Clark, Mary (36 yrs.)
Wife of William Clark
Died: May 24, 1847, of scurvy
Born: Jan. 2, 1847, North Carolina

Claton, James (23 yrs.)
  Husband of Lydia Claton
  Died: Nov. 28, 1847, of winter fever
  Born: May 23, 1824, Farington, Lancastershire, England

Clements, Alpheus G. (24 days)
  Son of Alven and Rhoda Clements
  Died: Feb. 26, 1847, of canker
  Born: Feb. 2, 1847, Winter Quarters

Clyne, Ann E. (3 mos.)
  Daughter of William and Betsey Clyne
  Died: Apr. 18, 1848
  Born: Jan. 8, 1848, Pottawatomie County, Iowa

Colbert, Nanvy (age not listed)
  No survivors listed
  Died: Oct. 12, 1847, of measles
  Born: No information given

Colbert, Sarah (7 yrs.)
  No survivors listed
  Died: Feb. 14, 1848
  Born: No information given

Collins, Charles H. (22 yrs.)
  Husband of Jane M. Collins
  Died: Nov. 26, 1847, of inflammation of lungs
  Born: Mar. 29, 1825, Adison County, Vt.

Conglin, _____ (1yr.)
  Son of Thomas and Mary Ett Conglin
  Died: Dec. 18, 1847, of canker
  Born: Sept. 16, 1846, De Calve County, Ill.

Connover, Evelina (39 yrs.)
  Wife of Peter Connover
  Died: Nov. 11, 1847, of typhus fever
  Born: May 20, 1806

Cook, Eliza H. (7 mos.)
  Daughter of Phineas W. and Eliza Cook
  Died: May 12, 1847, of inflammation of the bowels
  Born: Oct. 9, 1846, five miles below Winter Quarters

Cook, Joseph Y. (9 yrs.)
  Son of Aaron H. and Martha Cook
  Died: Dec. 23, 1846, of chills
  Born: Mar. 10, 1837, Ross County, Ohio

Cook, Louisa (35 yrs.)
  Wife of Aaron W. Cook
  Died: Nov. 16, 1846, of chills and fever, 12 miles up river from
    Winter Quarters
  Born: May, 1811, Maryland

Cook, Sharlot Aurelia (6 yrs.)
Daughter of Phineas and Ann Eliza Cook
Died: Nov. 22, 1847, of winter fever
Born: June 7, 1841, Kalamazoo County, Mich.

Corbit, Mary (82 yrs.)
Wife of James Corbit
Died: Sept. 2, 1847
Born: Farmington, Iowa

Corlass, Ellen (age not listed)
Daughter of Helen and Henry Corlass
Died: Jan. 10, 1847
Born: England

Corry, George (3 yrs.)
Son of George and Margaret Corry
Died: Sept. 18, 1846, of chills and fever
Born: May 1843, Portsmouth, N.H.

Coventon, Sarah A. (1 yr.)
Daughter of Robert and Elizabeth Coventon
Died: Oct. 16, 1846, of chills and fever
Born: Feb. 1, 1845, Oxford County, Miss.

Covert, Alma (1 yr.)
Son of William and Mary Covert
Died: Sept. 23, 1847, of typhus fever
Born: Feb. 4, 1846, Nauvoo, Ill.

Covey, Delica Ann (1 yr.)
Daughter of Benjamin and Diana Covey
Died: July 13, 1847, of consumption
Born: May 23, 1846, Van Buren County, Iowa

Covey, Diana (28 yrs.)
Wife of Benjamin Covey
Died: Dec. 9, 1847, of consumption
Born: May 28, 1819, Munroe County, N.Y.

Cox, Maria (3 yrs.)
Daughter of John and Eliza Cox
Died: Aug. 28, 1847, of fever
Born: Apr. 28, 1844, Nauvoo, Ill.

Cox, Philena (9 mos.)
Daughter of Amos and Philena Cox
Died: Dec. 23, 1846, of whooping cough
Born: Mar. 7, 1846, Nauvoo, Ill.

Cox, Phelina (1 yr.)
Daughter of Andrew J. and Elizabeth Ann Cox
Died: Sept. 26, 1846, of worms
Born: Oct. 6, 1844, Noxubee County, Miss.

Crookston, James (61 yrs.)
Husband of Mary Crookston
Died: Dec. 28, 1846
Born: Apr. 21, 1785, Tunnen, Scotland

Cummings, George A. (1 yr.)
Son of George and Jane Cummings
Died: Nov. 9, 1846, of chills and fever
Born: Feb. 17, 1845, Lima, Hancock County, Ill.

Cummings, Hariet (3 yrs.)
Daughter of George and Jane Cummings
Died: Apr. 18, 1847, of scurvy
Born: Nov. 23, 1843, Lima, Hancock County, Ill.

Cummings, James (77 yrs.)
Husband of Susannah Cummings
Died: Mar. 28, 1847, of scurvy
Born: Jan. 16, 1770, Dustable, Middlesec County, Mass.

Cummings, James Willard (2 mos.)
Son of James and Aura Annett Cummings
Died: Nov. 27, 1846
Born: Sept. 14, 1846, Cutler's Park

Cummings, John (4 yrs.)
Son of George and Jane Cummings
Died: Nov. 11, 1846, of chills and fever
Born: Jan. 13, 1842, Orline, Ind.

Cummings, Susannah (54 yrs.)
Wife of James Cummings
Died: Feb. 28, 1847, of consumption
Born: Mar. 3, 1792, Dunstable, Middlesex County, Mass.

Cutler, Sophrona (18 yrs.)
Daughter of Thaddeus and Emeline Cutler
Died: Oct. 1847, of typhus fever
Born: 1829, New York

Dalton, Martha T. (7 mos.)
Daughter of Charles and Mary E. Dalton
Died: May 9, 1847, of dropsy in the head
Born: Sept. 1846, Shell Creek, Iowa

Daniels, Francis A. (21 yrs.)
Wife of Cyrus Daniels
Died: Dec. 1, 1846, in childbed
Born: June 1, 1825, Birmingham, England

Daniels, Francis F. (1 day)
Daughter of Cyrus and Frances A. Daniels
Died: Dec. 1, 1846
Born: Dec. 1, 1846, Winter Quarters

Davidson, Joseph S. (9 yrs.)
Son of George W. and Nancy R. Davidson
Died: Mar. 17, 1848
Born: July 23, 1838, Far West, Mo.

Davis, Isaac (64 yrs.)
Husband of Edith Davis
Died: May 19, 1847, of bilious fever
Born: Feb. 18, 1783, New Jersey

Davis, Lydia (16 days)
Daughter of Franklin J. and Ann Davis
Died: Mar. 26, 1847
Born: Mar. 10, 1847, Winter Quarters

Dayton, Moses M. (16 yrs.)
Son of Hyrum Dayton
Died: Mar. 21, 1847
Born: Feb. 12, 1831, Geauga County, Ohio

Dewey, Ashabel (51 yrs.)
Husband of Harriet Dewey
Died: Oct. 6, 1846, of canker
Born: June 18, 1795

Dowdle, Robert (50 yrs.)
Husband of Sarah Dowdle
Died: Sept. 1, 1847, of lung fever
Born: Sept. 16, 1797, Pendleton Dist., S.C.

Duncan, Dolly H. (35 yrs.)
Wife of William A. Duncan
Died: Nov. 26, 1846
Born: Nov. 24, 1811, Christian County, Ky.

Duncan, William (43 yrs.)
Husband of Dolly H. Duncan
Died: Jan. 22, 1847, of dropsy
Born: Mar. 6, 1803, Roberson County, Tenn.

Dykes, Rachel (7 days)
Daughter of George P. and Synthy Dykes
Died: Jan. 13, 1847
Born: Jan. 6, 1847, Winter Quarters

Dykes, Synthy (46 yrs.)
Wife of George P. Dykes
Died: Jan. 11, 1847, of childbed fever
Born: Feb. 6, 1800, Saratoga County, N.Y.

Earl, Carolina (2 yrs.)
Daughter of Wilbur and Hariet Earl
Died: Apr. 19, 1847, of scarlet fever
Born: Jan. 9, 1845, Lee County, Iowa

Earl, Rhedana (2 yrs.)
Daughter of Sylvester and Laois C. Earl
Died: Dec. 21, 1847
Born: Aug. 18, 1845, Nauvoo, Ill.

Earl, Wilbur (11 mos.)
Son of Wilbur and Hariet Earl
Died: Apr. 13, 1847, of scarlet fever
Born: Apr. 29, 1846, Garden Grove, Iowa

Eddins, George (38 yrs.)
No survivors listed
Died: Apr. 26, 1847
Born: 1809, Herefordshire, England

Edwards, Maria Elizabeth (32 yrs.)
Wife of Elisha Edwards
Died: June 30, 1847, of consumption
Born: July 4, 1814

Eggleston, Samuel (7 mos.)
Son of Samuel and Lurania Eggleston
Died: Aug. 23, 1847, of summer complaint
Born: Jan. 16, 1847, Winter Quarters

Eldrige, Helen Louise (2 mos.)
Daughter of Horace and Betsey Eldrige
Died: Aug. 30, 1847, of canker
Born: June 8, 1847, Winter Quarters

Empey, Brigham (6 yrs.)
Son of William and Maria Empey
Died: Sept. 2, 1847, of measles
Born: No information given

Ensign, Horas (49 yrs.)
Husband of Mary B. Ensign
Died: Sept. 26, 1847, of chills and fever
Born: Sept. 28, 1797, Westfield, Mass.

Fairbanks, Joseph (68 yrs.)
No survivors listed
Died: Feb. 25, 1846, of chills and fever
Born: Oct. 15, 1778, Worcester County, Mass.

Fauset, William (3 yrs.)
Son of William and Matilda Fauset
Died: Oct. 5, 1847, of canker
Born: Oct. 6, 1844, Nauvoo, Ill.

Felshaw, Anna M. (8 yrs.)
Daughter of J. William and Mariah Felshaw
Died: Jan. 15, 1848, of winter fever
Born: Dec. 28, 1839, Nauvoo, Ill.

Fielding, Hyrum (4 mos.)
    Son of Joseph and Hannah Fielding
    Died: Aug. 4, 1847
    Born: Apr. 4, 1847, Winter Quarters

Flake, Frederick (1 day)
    Son of James M. and Agnes H. Flake
    Died: Nov. 3, 1846
    Born: Nov. 3, 1846, Cutler's Park

Flake, Samuel B. (5 mos.)
    Son of James M. and Agnes H. Flake
    Died: Mar. 25, 1847
    Born: Oct. 12, 1846, Cutler's Park

Foster, Thomas (57 yrs.)
    No survivors listed
    Died: Sept. 28, 1847, of typhus fever
    Born: June 18, 1790

Gardner, Emma (47 yrs.)
    Wife of Elias Gardner
    Died: Nov. 25, 1846, of canker
    Born: Aug. 14, 1799, Christian County, Ky.

Gardner, Genet (3 yrs.)
    Daughter of William and Genet Gardner
    Died: Sept. 14, 1846
    Born: July 14, 1843

Garner, Silva (1 yr.)
    Daughter of William and Sarah Garner
    Died: Sept. 13, 1847, of fever
    Born: Aug. 13, 1846, Nauvoo, Ill.

Gates, Caroline E. (age not given)
    Wife of Jacob Gates
    Died: Sept. 15, 1846, of consumption

Gates, Mary E. (7 mos.)
    Daughter of Jacob and Caroline Gates
    Died: May 3, 1847, of consumption
    Born: Oct. 2, 1846, Winter Quarters

Glasgow, Josinnah (35 yrs.)
    Wife of Samuel Glasgow
    Died: June 20, 1847, of dropsy
    Born: Apr. 19, 1812, Ireland

Glines, James E. (1 yr.)
    Son of James and Elizabeth Glines
    Died: Oct. 22, 1847, of canker
    Born: Nov. 1846, Punkah County

Godart, ———
Wife of Stephen Godart
Died: 1847, of scurvy
Born: No information given

Godfrey, Eliza Jane (6 mos.)
Daughter of Joseph and Ann Eliza Godfrey
Died: July 8, 1847, of diarrhea
Born: Dec. 14, 1846, Winter Quarters

Gouldsmith, David (4 yrs.)
Son of Gilbert D. and Abigail Gouldsmith
Died: Sept. 18, 1846, of chills and fever
Born: May 1842, Nauvoo, Ill.

Grant, Heber C. (3 mos.)
Son of George and Margaret S. Grant
Died: Dec. 13, 1846
Born: Sept. 13, 1846, Cutler's Park

Grant, Loisa M. (23 yrs.)
Wife of George D. Grant
Died: Dec. 30, 1846
Born: Apr. 17, 1823, Hiram Township, Portage County, Ohio

Grant, Mary Ann (26 yrs.)
Wife of David Grant
Died: Feb. 1, 1847
Born: Sept. 18, 1820, York, Livingston County, N.Y.

Grover, Sarah Jane (1 yr.)
Daughter of Joseph and Sally Grover
Died: Nov. 16, 1846, of chills
Born: Mar. 2, 1845, Ohio

Guley, Henereta (1 yr.)
Daughter of Samuel and Avanda Guley
Died: Aug. 29, 1847, of consumption
Born: Mar. 4, 1846, Nauvoo, Ill.

Hakes, Patty C. (17 yrs.)
Daughter of Weeden V. and Eliza A. Hakes
Died: Oct. 9, 1846, of chills and fever
Born: Oct. 2, 1829, Columbia County, N.Y.

Harmon, Anny (54 yrs.)
Wife of Jessy P. Harmon
Died: Jan. 16, 1847, of chills and fever
Born: Mar. 6, 1792, New Ashford, Berkshire County, Mass.

Harmon, Appleton (1 yr.)
Son of Appleton and Elmira Harmon
Died: Sept. 22, 1847, of bowel complaint
Born: Sept. 23, 1846, Cutler's Park

Harper, Ellen (1 yr.)
Daughter of Charles and Lavinia Harper
Died: Aug. 29, 1847, of summer complaint
Born: Apr. 16, 1846, Nauvoo, Ill.

Harris, Priscilla (30 yrs.)
Wife of Walter Harris
Died: Feb. 1, 1847, of bilious colic
Born: Aug. 12, 1816, Herefordshire, England

Harris, Robert (5 mos.)
Son of Robert and Maria Harris
Died: July 30, 1847
Born: Feb. 3, 1847, Winter Quarters

Harrison, Sabina Ann (28 yrs.)
Wife of Isaac Harrison
Died: Feb. 24, 1847
Born: Jan. 8, 1819, Columbia County, Ohio

Hart, Harriet A. (13 days)
Daughter of Joseph and Clarissa Hart
Died: Jan. 12, 1847
Born: Dec. 31, 1846, Winter Quarters

Harvey, Adelia
Daughter of John and Eliza Harvey
Died: Mar. 16, 1848, stillborn
Born: Mar. 16, 1848, Winter Quarters

Hatch, Abigail (48 yrs.)
Wife of Israel Hatch
Died: Feb. 12, 1847
Born: Dec. 12, 1798, Elizabeth, Upper Canada

Hatch, Elizabeth (74 yrs.)
Wife of Jeremiah Hatch
Died: Dec. 16, 1847
Born: April 27, 1773

Heath, Barbary (52 yrs.)
Wife of John Heath
Died: Oct. 21, 1846, of chills and fever
Born: 1794, Eteny, Staffordshire, England

Hess, Amanda (15 yrs.)
Daughter of Peter M. and Mary Hess
Died: Aug. 28, 1847, of fever
Born: Apr. 6, 1832, Philadelphia, Pa.

Hickerson, Joseph (2 yrs.)
Son of George W. and Sarah Hickerson
Died: Nov. 19, 1847
Born: Mar. 11, 1845, Nauvoo, Ill.

Hill, Charles (18 yrs.)
Son of Leonard and Sally Hill
Died: May 6, 1847, of chills and fever
Born: Jan. 6, 1829

Hill, Isabella (25 yrs.)
Wife of Archibald Hill
Died: Mar. 20, 1847
Born: July 8, 1821

Hill, Sally (39 yrs.)
Wife of Leonard Hill
Died: Feb. 15, 1847
Born: Mar. 14, 1808

Holman, Joshua S. (52 yrs.)
Husband of Rebecca W. Holman
Died: Nov. 1, 1846
Born: Apr. 12, 1794, Templeton, Worcester County, Mass.

Holmes, Lucy Elvira (1 yr.)
Daughter of Jonathan and Martha Holmes
Died: June 1, 1847
Born: Oct. 11, 1845, Nauvoo, Ill.

Horlick, Julia (1 yr.)
Daughter of John and Elizabeth Horlick
Died: Sept. 2, 1847, of fever
Born: Aug. 2, 1846, Nauvoo, Ill.

Houston, Mary (63 yrs.)
Wife of James Houston
Died: Mar. 26, 1847, of scurvy
Born: Oct. 2, 1783, Bucks County, Pa.

Hovey, _____ (1 yr.)
Daughter of Orlando and Abigail Hovey
Died: Jan. 14, 1848, of measles
Born: Jan. 23, 1846, Nauvoo, Ill.

Hovey, Jane (2 yrs.)
Daughter of Joseph and Martha Hovey
Died: Jan. 19, 1848, of measles
Born: June 17, 1845, Nauvoo, Ill.

Hovey, Martha A. (32 yrs.)
Wife of Joseph Hovey
Died: Sept. 16, 1846, of bilious fever
Born: 1814, Portsmouth, N.H.

Hoytes, Jsie C. (16 days)
Son of Jsie C. and Eliza Hoytes
Died: Dec. 5, 1845, of inflammation
Born: Nov. 19, 1846, Winter Quarters

Huls, Lewis S.
Died: Mar. 21, 1847 of scurvy
Born: No information given

Hunter, Carolina Roccaly (6 days)
Daughter of Edward and Laura Alvina Hunter
Died: Oct. 22, 1846
Born: Oct. 16, 1846, Cutler's Park

Jacob (23 yrs.)
Negro servant of John Bankhead
Died: Apr. 7, 1847, of winter fever
Born: Oct. 1823, Monroe County, Miss.

Jenne, Brigham (1 yr.)
Son of Benjamin and Sally Jenne
Died: Dec. 1, 1847, of inflammation of the lungs
Born: Jan. 25, 1846, Cook County, Ill.

Jones, Hannah
Wife of Alonzo Jones
Died: No dates given, buried at Cutler's Park

Jones, Jane (1 mo.)
Daughter of Richard Watson and Ann Jones
Died: Apr. 15, 1847
Born: Mar. 6, 1847, Winter Quarters

Jones, Mary (9 yrs.)
Daughter of William and Elizabeth Jones
Died: Dec. 7, 1846, of chills
Born: June 25, 1837, Portsmouth, Ohio

Kay, John (1 yr.)
Son of John and Ellen Kay
Died: July 20, 1847, of summer complaint
Born: Feb. 11, 1846, Nauvoo, Ill.

Keley, Brigham (1 yr.)
Son of Eli and Lutitia Keley (name probably Kelsey, see below)
Died: Aug. 28, 1847, of chills and fever
Born: May 26, 1846, Nauvoo, Ill.

Kelley, William Thaddeus (8 mos.)
Son of Alvey and Rosey Kelley
Died: Sept. 15, 1846
Born: Jan. 12, 1846, Nauvoo, Ill.

Kelsey, Melissa (5 yrs.)
Daughter of Stephen and Rachel Kelsey
Died: Oct. 30, 1846
Born: Feb. 17, 1841, Montville, Gage County, Ohio

Kelsey, Minervia M. (4 yrs.)
Daughter of Eli B. and Lutitia Kelsey
Died: Nov. 25, 1847, of canker
Born: May 10, 1843, Trumble County, Ky.

Kimball, Rachel (1 yr.)
Daughter of Heber C. Kimball and Lucy R. Kimball
Died: Dec. 29, 1847, of canker
Born: Jan. 25, 1846, Nauvoo, Ill.

Kimball, Sophrony (22 yrs.)
Wife of Heber C. Kimball
Died: Jan. 24, 1847, of chills and fever
Born: Apr. 5, 1824, Erie County, Pa.

King, Elizabeth (70 yrs.)
Wife of Thomas King
Died: Sept. 13, 1847, of chills
Born: 1777

Knights, Orpha (1 yr.)
Son of Cornelius and Permelia Knights
Died: Oct. 28, 1847, of canker
Born: Dec. 24, 1845, Nauvoo, Ill.

Knowls, John (age not given)
Husband of Hannah Knowls
Died: Apr. 8, 1847, of scurvy
Born: No information given

Lamb, Robert P. (1 yr.)
Son of Benjamin P. and Elizabeth Lamb
Died: Nov. 21, 1846, of chills
Born: May 2, 1845, Nauvoo, Ill.

Lance, William J. (3 mos.)
Son of Jacob and Mary Jane Lance
Died: Apr. 12, 1847
Born: Jan. 16, 1847, Winter Quarters

Lawrence, Angelina Elizabeth (3 yrs.)
Daughter of John and Rhoda Lawrence
Died: Oct. 22, 1846
Born: Oct. 27, 1843, Adams County, Ill.

Lawrence, John (14 days)
Son of John and Rhoda Lawrence
Died: Mar. 11, 1847
Born: Feb. 25, 1847, Winter Quarters

Lawrence, John (43 yrs.)
Husband of Rhoda Lawrence
Died: Dec. 13, 1846
Born: June 21, 1803, Duchess County, N.Y.

Lawrence, Rhoda Almira (1 yr.)
Daughter of John and Rhoda Lawrence
Died: Oct. 25, 1846
Born: Mar. 9, 1845, Hancock County, Ill.

Lemon, Frances (62 yrs.)
Wife of James Lemon
Died: Oct. 22, 1847, of burns
Born: 1785, Scotland

Leonard, Ezra (1 day)
Son of Truman and Ortentia Leonard
Died: Nov. 4, 1846, stillborn
Born: Nov. 4, 1846, Winter Quarters

Littleton, Mary Ann (14 yrs.)
Orphan
Died: May 14, 1848
Born: July 13, 1833, St. Francisville, Mo.

Lott, Harriet A. (11 yrs.)
Daughter of Cornelius and Permelia Lott
Died: Oct. 5, 1847, of fever
Born: Mar. 30, 1836, Susquehannah County, Pa.

Lott, Joseph D. (7 yrs.)
Son of Cornelius and Permelia Lott
Died: Oct. 15, 1847
Born: Feb. 18, 1839, Dayton, Ohio

Lott, Lyman C. (2 mos.)
Son of John and Mary Ann Lott
Died: Dec. 14, 1847, of fever
Born: Sept. 24, 1847, Winter Quarters

Lowell, William (13 days)
Son of John and Ann Lowell
Died: Feb. 28, 1847
Born: Feb. 15, 1847, Winter Quarters

Luce, Thomas Benton (10 yrs.)
Son of Ephraim and Lydia Luce
Died: Oct. 21, 1847, of measles
Born: Apr. 21, 1837

Luty, Nathan H. (4 yrs.)
Son of Albert and Susannah Luty
Died: Dec. 4, 1846, of canker
Born: Aug. 6, 1842, Philadelphia, Pa.

Lyman, Don Carlos (5 mos.)
Son of Amsy and Eliza M. Lyman
Died: Dec. 12, 1846
Born: July 14, 1846, Omaha Nation, Camp of Israel

Lytle, Sarah (73 yrs.)
No survivors listed
Died: June 5, 1847, killed by wagon
Born: May 10, 1774, Carlisle, Pa.

Mabery, Rebecca (8 mos.)
Daughter of David and Rebecca Mabery
Died: June 6, 1847, of lung complaint
Born: Sept. 23, 1846, Bonneport, Van Buren County, Iowa

Mangum, Beely Franklin (3 yrs.)
Son of Joseph and Emeline Mangum
Died: Oct. 10, 1847, of measles
Born: Oct. 10, 1844, Mississippi

Mangum, Rebecca (60 yrs.)
Wife of John Mangum
Died: Feb. 23, 1847

Mann, Ann E. (40 yrs.)
Daughter of Samuel and Mary Mann
Died: Jan. 13, 1847, of canker
Born: May 23, 1806, Providence, R.I.

Martin, Edward (4 mos.)
Son of Edward and Alis Martin
Died: Sept. 6, 1847, of ague
Born: Apr. 11, 1847, Winter Quarters

Martin, Edward John (7 mos.)
Son of Edward and Alis Martin
Died: July 14, 1848, of dysentery
Born: Nov. 28, 1847, Nauvoo, Ill.

McCord, Hirum (1 yr.)
Son of Alexander and Syble McCord
Died: Oct. 25, 1846
Born: June 7, 1845

McCoulough, Clarinda
Wife of Levi McCoulough
Died: July 13, 1847, of consumption
Born: No information given

McCullough, Faley Jerusha (2 yrs.)
Daughter of Levi and Clarinda McCullough
Died: Aug. 2, 1847, of consumption
Born: July 10, 1845, Jackson County, Mich.

McDonald, Washington (11 yrs.)
Son of John and Rachel McDonald
Died: June 25, 1847
Born: Aug. 9, 1835, Philadelphia, Pa.

McGate, Lucy T. (26 yrs.)
Wife of James McGate
Died: Mar. 18, 1847, of consumption
Born: Sept. 23, 1820, Otsego County, N.Y.

Melvil, Elizabeth (25 yrs.)
Wife of Alexander Melvil
Died: Nov., 1846, of chills and canker
Born: Dec. 20, 1820, Fifeshire, Scotland

Mitchell, Elisa (40 yrs.)
Wife of William C. Mitchell
Died: Jan. 1, 1847
Born: Mar. 11, 1806, York, Yorkshire, England

Mitchell, Persis (11 mos.)
Daughter of Benjamin T. and Lovina Mitchell
Died: Nov. 19, 1846, of inflammation of lungs
Born: Nov. 26, 1845, Nauvoo, Ill.

Morley, Lucy (61 yrs.)
Wife of Isaac Morley
Died: Jan. 3, 1848, of winter fever
Born: Jan. 24, 1786, Montague, Hanshire County, Mass.

Morse, William A. (1 mo.)
Son of Gilbert and Synthy Morse
Died: Mar. 7, 1847
Born: Feb. 5, 1847, Winter Quarters

Neeley, Elizabeth (38 yrs.)
Wife of Lewis Neeley
Died: Feb. 2, 1847
Born: Apr. 9, 1808, Colerane County, N.Y.

Neeley, Elizabeth (6 mos.)
Daughter of Lewis and Elizabeth Neeley
Died: Aug. 3, 1847, of summer complaint
Born: Jan. 25, 1847, Council Bluffs, Iowa

Neff, Cyrus (20 yrs.)
Son of John and Mary Neff
Died: Mar. 4, 1847, of fever
Born: Jan. 16, 1827, Strasburg Pt., Lancaster County, Pa.

Neibour, _____
Daughter of Alexander and Ellen Neibour
Died: Dec. 12, 1847, stillborn
Born: Dec. 12, 1847, Winter Quarters

Noah, Pleasant D. (31 yrs.)
Husband of Martha Ann Noah
Died: Dec. 2, 1846, of chills
Born: Apr. 7, 1815, Tennessee

Noble, Hyrum B. (1 yr.)
Son of Joseph B. and Mary A. Noble
Died: Nov. 5, 1846, of chills and dropsy
Born: May 6, 1845, Nauvoo, Ill.

Noble, Sarah (27 yrs.)
Wife of Joseph B. Noble
Died: Dec. 28, 1846
Born: Oct. 19, 1819, Lynn, Essex County, Mass.

Oakey, Eliza (27 yrs.)
Wife of Edward Oakey
Died: Apr. 21, 1847, of scurvy
Born: May 9, 1819, Herefordshire, England

Olmstead, Alonzo (9 yrs.)
Son of Philip and Corinth Olmstead
Died: Jan. 4, 1848, of canker
Born: Feb. 18, 1838, Bethel, Branch County, Mich.

Olmstead, Mary Jane (1 yr.)
Daughter of Philip and Corintha Olmstead
Died: Oct. 22, 1847, of measles
Born: Jan. 19, 1846, Montrose, Iowa

Orton, James (7 mos.)
Son of Elias and Louise Orton
Died: Sept. 30, 1847
Born: Feb. 1847, Winter Quarters

Ott, Frederick D (2 yrs.)
Son of Frederick and Nancy Ott
Died: Feb. 24, 1847
Born: July 23, 1844, Nauvoo, Ill.

Owen, Lydia (35 yrs.)
Wife of Seeley Owen
Died: Sept. 19, 1846, of fever
Born: 1811, Vermont

Packer, Sarah Elizabeth (1 yr.)
Daughter of Jonathan and Angelina Packer
Died: Dec. 9, 1846, of chills
Born: Oct. 19, 1845, Nauvoo, Ill.

Parcket, Charles (6 days)
Son of Charles and Achsah Parcket
Died: Oct. 25, 1846
Born: Oct. 19, 1846, Winter Quarters

Patten, John (60 yrs.)
Husband of Hannah Patten
Died: Apr. 12, 1847, of scurvy
Born: Mar. 14, 1787, New Hampshire

Patten, Rachel (2 yrs.)
Daughter of Charles and Peggy Patten
Died: Sept. 13, 1847, of measles
Born: Mar. 13, 1845, Nauvoo, Ill.

Pearce, Mary H. (25 yrs.)
Daughter of Robert and Hannah Pearce
(Believed to have been plural wife of Brigham Young. In *Manuscript History of Brigham Young* he writes "March 16, 1847, I buried my wife, Mary H. Pearce, age 25 years, daughter of Robert and Hannah Pearce. She died of pneumonia.")
Died: Mar. 16, 1847
Born: Nov. 29, 1821, Chester County, Pa.

Pearson, Ephraim (60 yrs.)
Husband of Rody Pearson
Died: Nov. 21, 1846, of chills and dysentery
Born: Apr. 28, 1787, Vermont

Pearson, Henry (16 yrs.)
Son of Ephraim J. and Rhoda Pearson
Died: Nov. 6, 1846, of dysentery
Born: May 23, 1830, Oneida County, N.Y.

Pendleton, Emeline (2 yrs.)
Daughter of Calvin C. and Sally Ann Pendleton
Died: Mar. 24, 1847, of congestive fever
Born: Dec. 15, 1844, Nauvoo, Ill.

Pendleton, Permelia (7 mos.)
Son of Joseph Thomas and Mary Emeline Pendleton
Died: Aug. 17, 1847, of bowel complaint
Born: Jan. 5, 1847, Winter Quarters

Pendleton, Silvy A. (29 yrs.)
Wife of Calvin C. Pendleton
Died: Sept. 13, 1846, of canker
Born: Oct. 10, 1816, Lincoln County, Maine

Petty, John B (9 yrs.)
Son of Albert and Catherine Petty
Died: Feb. 6, 1847, of chills
Born: Apr. 21, 1837, Far West, Mo.

Phippen, Isaac E. (1 yr.)
Son of Joseph F. and Ann Phippen
Died: Jan. 1, 1848, of canker
Born: Dec. 17, 1846, Nauvoo, Ill.

Pierce, Dorothy (age not given)
Died: Nov. 16, 1846
Born: Chester County, Pa.

Pierson, Mary M. (7 yrs.)
Daughter of Amous L. and Druzilla Pierson
Died: Jan. 1, 1848, of canker
Born: July 23, 1840, Rutherford, Tenn.

Pitt, Cornelia M. (1 yr.)
Daughter of William and Cornelia M. Pitt
Died: Apr. 17, 1847
Born: Sept. 12, 1845, Nauvoo, Ill.

Pixton, Robert Holeman (1 mo.)
Son of Robert and Elizabeth Pixton
Died: Nov. 18, 1846
Born: Oct. 3, 1846, Winter Quarters

Pond, Abigail A. (18 yrs.)
Daughter of Stillman and Almira Pond
Died: Dec. 7, 1846, of chills
Born: July 14, 1828, Hubardston, Worcester County, Mass.

Pond, Almira (34 yrs.)
Wife of Stillman Pond
Died: May 17, 1847, of consumption
Born: 1813, Worcester County, Mass.

Pond, Harriet M. (11 yrs.)
Daughter of Stillman and Mariah Pond
Died: Dec. 4, 1846, of chills
Born: Sept. 6, 1835, Hubardston, Worcester County, Mass.

Pond, Laury Jane (14 yrs.)
Daughter of Stillman and Almira Pond
Died: Dec. 2, 1846, of chills and fever
Born: Mar. 8, 1832, Westminster, Worcester County, Mass.

Pond, Lyman (6 yrs.)
Son of Stillman and Mariah Pond
Died: Jan. 15, 1847, of chills
Born: Apr. 24, 1840, New Salem, Franklin County, Mass.

Porter, Amy (32 yrs.)
Wife of Chancy W. Porter
Died: Apr. 6, 1847, of scurvy
Born: Feb. 22, 1815, Kings Creek County, Ohio

Porter, Benjamin (1 day)
Son of Chancy W. and Emma Porter
Died: Dec. 12, 1846
Born: Dec. 11, 1846, Winter Quarters

Porter, Joseph (1 day)
Son of Chancy W. and Emma Porter
Died: Dec. 12, 1846
Born: Dec. 11, 1846, Winter Quarters

Potter, Gardner G.
Son of Gardner and Eveline Potter
Died: Mar. 13, 1848, stillborn
Born: Mar. 13, 1848, Winter Quarters

Pratt, Vanson (1 yr.)
Son of Orson and Sarah M. Pratt
Died: July 28, 1847, of dropsy of the brain
Born: Jan. 23, 1846, Nauvoo, Ill.

Proctor, John (83 yrs.)
Husband of Elizabeth Proctor
Died: Mar. 18, 1847, of old age
Born: Jan. 1765, Pennsylvania

Proctor, John (29 yrs.)
No survivors given
Died: Sept. 24, 1846, of chills and fever
Born: 1818, Preston, England

Pulsiver, Henry (1 yr.)
Son of Elias and Polly Pulsiver
Died: Dec. 7, 1847, of lung complaint
Born: Mar. 15, 1846, Nauvoo, Ill.

Putney, Gerry (38 yrs.)
Husband of Eley Putney
Died: Apr. 15, 1847, of scurvy
Born: Mar. 17, 1809, Charlton, Worcester County, Mass.

Ralston, Augustus P. (1 yr.)
Son of John and Hannah Ralston
Died: Dec. 6, 1846, of chills
Born: Aug. 7, 1845, Chester County, Pa.

Randall, Henry (65 yrs.)
Husband of Sally Randall
Died: Mar. 8, 1849, of consumption
Born: Jan. 26, 1784, Rhode Island

Reaves, James Coiley (1 yr.)
Son of Coiley Reaves
Died: Aug. 13, 1847, of summer complaint
Born: June 22, 1846, Council Bluffs, Iowa

Reaves, Marthy (17 yrs.)
Wife of Sealy Reaves
Died: Feb. 24, 1847
Born: Mar. 20, 1829, Hartland, Niagara County, N.Y.

Redding, Joseph C. (1 yr.)
Son of Jackson and Martha Redding
Died: Aug. 17, 1847, of bowel complaint
Born: Feb. 24, 1846, Sugar Creek, Iowa

Redding, Marthy M. (22 yrs.)
Wife of Jackson Redding
Died: Mar. 15, 1847
Born: June 23, 1825, Upper Canada

Remington, Sally (56 yrs.)
Wife of Joseph Remington
Died: July 28, 1847, of consumption
Born: May 15, 1791, White Hall, N.Y.

Richards, Elizabeth (17 yrs.)
Wife of Franklin Richards
Died: Mar. 29, 1847, of scurvy
Born: Oct. 28, 1829, Pennsylvania

Richards, Wealthy Lovisa (2 yrs.)
Daughter of Franklin and Jane S. Richards
Died: Sept. 14, 1846
Born: Nov. 2, 1843, Nauvoo, Ill.

Richardson, Loly Ann (1 yr.)
Daughter of E. C. and A. R. Richardson
Died: Aug. 17, 1847

Riche, _____ (only information on gravesite)

Robersen, Susan A. (3 mos.)
Daughter of Joseph L. and Susan Robersen
Died: Mar. 12, 1847
Born: Nov. 15, 1846, Winter Quarters

Roberson, William (44 yrs.)
Husband of Elizabeth Roberson
Died: Nov. 27, 1846
Born: July 6, 1802, Charleston, Montgomery County, N.Y.

Roberts, Charles D. (4 yrs.)
Son of Horace and Harriet Roberts
Died: Apr. 26, 1848, drowned
Born: Oct. 14, 1843, Nauvoo, Ill.

Rolfe, David L. (5 days)
Son of Samuel and Elizabeth Rolfe
Died: Nov. 6, 1846
Born: Nov. 1, 1846, Winter Quarters

Rollins, Ephraim A. (2 yrs.)
Son of James H. and Evelina Rollins
Died: Aug. 19, 1847, of inflammation of the bowels
Born: July 7, 1845, Nauvoo, Ill.

Roundy, Joannah (22 yrs.)
Wife of Loring H. Roundy
Died: Feb. 5, 1847, of canker
Born: Nov. 27, 1824, Benson, Rutland County, Vt.

Rushton, Isabella H. (1 yr.)
Daughter of John and Margaret Rushton
Died: Dec. 3, 1846, of canker
Born: Sept. 15, 1845, Nauvoo, Ill.

Sanders, Elisy Jane (3 yrs.)
Daughter of Moses M. and Amanda Sanders
Died: Apr. 4, 1847
Born: June 23, 1843, Nauvoo, Ill.

Sheets, Margaret (3 mos.)
Daughter of Elijah F. and Margaret Sheets
Died: Apr. 14, 1847
Born: Dec. 25, 1846, Winter Quarters

Sheets, Margaret (27 yrs.)
Wife of Elijah F. Sheets
Died: Feb. 1, 1847, of canker
Born: July 3, 1819, New Radner, Herefordshire, England

Shumway, Harriet (3 yrs.)
Daughter of Charles and July Ann Shumway
Died: Apr. 13, 1847, of canker
Born: Feb. 10, 1844, Nauvoo, Ill.

Shumway, Julia Ann (38 yrs.)
Wife of Charles Shumway
Died: Nov. 15, 1846, of chills and fever
Born: Nov. 28, 1807, Shubridge, Worcester County, Mass.

Sirrine, Mephiboseth (36 yrs.)
No survivors listed
Died: April 29, 1848, of consumption, aboard steamer *Niagara*, on
Ohio River, returning from mission to England. Buried at Nauvoo,
then re-interred at Winter Quarters, May 8, 1848.
Born: Oct. 27, 1811, Phillipstown, N.Y.

Skeen, Joseph (2 yrs.)
Son of Joseph and Maria Amanda Skeen
Died: Aug. 20, 1847, of consumption
Born: Apr. 12, 1845, Hancock County, Ill.

Smith, Caroline (5 yrs.)
Daughter of Ira and Louisa Smith
Died: Aug. 10, 1847, of fever and ague
Born: Oct. 15, 1841, Greenburg, Iowa

Smith, David Kimball (1 yr.)
Son of Heber and Sarah Kimble Smith
Died: Aug. 18, 1847, of cholera
Born: Mar. 6, 1846, near Richardson's Point, Iowa

Smith, Don Carlos (10 mos.)
Son of George A. and Lucy Smith
Died: July 21, 1847, of diarrhea
Born: Sept. 11, 1846, Cutler's Park

Smith, John (9 hrs.)
Son of George A. and Bathsheba Smith
Died: Apr. 4, 1847
Born: Apr. 4, 1847, Winter Quarters

Smith, Nancy A. (1 yr.)
Daughter of George A. and Anny Smith
Died: Apr. 17, 1847
Born: Mar. 23, 1846, Nauvoo, Ill.

Smith, Nancy Clement (31 yrs.)
Daughter of James and Betsy Clement
Died: Mar. 27, 1847, of scurvy
Born: Oct. 31, 1815, Thompson County, N.Y.

Smith, William (48 yrs.)
Husband of Ann Smith
Died: Jan. 29, 1847, of chills
Born: Nov. 1798, Lancastershire, England

Smoot, _____ (4 mos.)
Abraham Smoot's sister's child
Died: Apr. 29, 1847, of consumption
Born: Dec. 5, 1846, Winter Quarters

Snow, Mary Minervy (10 mos.)
Daughter of Erastus and Minerva Snow
Died: Aug. 1, 1847, of summer complaint
Born: Oct. 1, 1846, at Winter Quarters

Snyder, Olive (1 yr.)
Daughter of Chester and Catherine Snyder
Died: June 6, 1847, of inflammation of the bowels
Born: Feb. 26, 1846, Nauvoo, Ill.

Spears, Elizabeth (21 days)
Daughter of George and Sarah Spears
Died: Oct. 31, 1846
Born: Oct. 10, 1846, Cutler's Park

Spears, George (47 yrs.)
Husband of Sarah N. Spears
Died: Nov. 12, 1846
Born: Oct. 1799, Birkshire County, Scotland

Spears, Mary (5 days)
Daughter of William and Genet Spears
Died: Nov. 7, 1846
Born: Nov. 2, 1846, Cutler's Park

Spears, William (53 yrs.)
    Husband of Genet Spears
    Died: Mar. 7, 1847, of black leg
    Born: May 4, 1793, Scotland

Spicer, Abney (23 yrs.)
    Wife of John Spicer
    Died: May 21, 1847, of chills and fever
    Born: Dec. 31, 1824, Cayuga County, N.Y.

Sprague, Abigail (74 yrs.)
    Wife of Hezekiah Sprague
    Died: Jan. 22, 1847, of old age
    Born: July 18, 1772, Sheffield, Conn.

Sprague, Mary Eliza Annetta (3 mos.)
    Daughter of Samuel L. and Mary W. Sprague
    Died: Apr. 23, 1848, of whooping cough
    Born: Jan. 20, 1848, Winter Quarters

Stevenson, Catherine (77 yrs.)
    No survivors listed
    Died: Apr. 14, 1847, of scurvy
    Born: 1770, Lancastershire, England

Stillman, Dexter (4 mos.)
    Son of Dexter and Barbery Stillman
    Died: July 28, 1847, of consumption
    Born: Mar. 16, 1847, Winter Quarters

Stout, Elisabeth (24 yrs.)
    Wife of Allen Stout
    Died: Jan. 30, 1848, of childbed fever
    Born: Oct. 30, 1823, Rutherford County, Tenn.

Stout, Louisa (1 yr.)
    Daughter of Hosea and Louisa Stout
    Died: Aug. 5, 1847, of bowel complaint
    Born: Apr. 22, 1846, Garden Grove, Iowa

Stout, Marinda (20 yrs.)
    Wife of Hosea Stout
    Died: Sept. 26, 1846, of dropsy
    Born: Aug. 20, 1826, Bedford County, Tenn.

Stow, Either (10 yrs.)
    Son of James P. and Jemima Stow
    Died: Sept. 29, 1847, of scurvy
    Born: Sept. 11, 1837, Wain County, Ohio

Swap, Agnes (3 mos.)
    Daughter of William and Elizabeth Swap
    Died: Sept. 16, 1846, of chills and fever
    Born: June 16, 1846, Pottawatomie nation

Sweet, Mary Ann (31 yrs.)
   Wife of George Sweet
   Died: Nov. 18, 1847, of measles
   Born: Oct. 3, 1816, Upper Canada

Tanner, Centhia Marie (2 yrs.)
   Daughter of John and Rebecca Tanner
   Died: May 22, 1847, of dropsy
   Born: Mar. 14, 1845, Lee County, Iowa

Tanner, Louisa (35 yrs.)
   Wife of Sidney Tanner
   Died: Sept. 19, 1846, of fever
   Born: Feb. 5, 1811, Washington County, N.Y.

Tanner, Mason A. (4 mos.)
   Son of Sidney and Louisa Tanner
   Died: Nov. 30, 1846, of chills and canker
   Born: July 8, 1846, Council Bluffs, Iowa

Taylor, Mary R. (89 yrs.)
   Wife of Thomas Taylor
   Died: Dec. 2, 1847, of old age
   Born: April 1758, New York

Tenney, George A. (6 yrs.)
   Son of Nathan A. and Olive Tenney
   Died: May 1, 1848, of nervous fever
   Born: June 21, 1841, Davis City, Ill.

Thane, Jane (13 yrs.)
   Daughter of Savin and Lavina Thane
   Died: Sept. 28, 1847, of measles
   Born: Sept. 23, 1834, New York state

Thatcher, Hesikiah Jr. (15 hrs.)
   Son of Hesikiah and Abbey Thatcher
   Died: Mar. 11, 1847
   Born: Mar. 11, 1847, Winter Quarters

Thomas, Daniel (38 yrs.)
   Husband of Margaret Thomas
   Died: Jan. 25, 1848, of consumption
   Born: Dec. 6, 1809, South Carolina

Thomas, Morgan E. (20 yrs.)
   Son of Daniel and Martha P. Thomas
   Died: Feb. 8, 1847, of consumption
   Born: Dec. 7, 1826, Sonor County, Middle Tenn.

Tibbitts, Alva (38 yrs.)
   Husband of Caroline Tibbitts
   Died: Oct. 24, 1847, of summer complaint
   Born: Mar. 12, 1809, Lawrency County, N.Y.

Turley, Frances (47 yrs.)
Wife of Theodore Turley
Died: Aug. 30, 1847, of scurvy
Born: Jan. 22, 1800, Birmingham, England

Turley, Hyrum O. (4 mos.)
Son of Theodore and Ellen Turley
Died: Apr. 29, 1847, of croup
Born: Dec. 5, 1846, Winter Quarters

Turley, Joseph Smith (3 mos.)
Son of Theodore and Ellen Turley
Died: Mar. 5, 1847, of water on the brain
Born: Dec. 5, 1846, Winter Quarters

Turley, Princette (2 yrs.)
Daughter of Theodore and Sara Ellen Turley
Died: Sept. 6, 1847, of fever
Born: Aug. 2, 1845, Nauvoo, Ill.

Turley, Sarah Ellen (29 yrs.)
Wife of Theodore Turley
Died: May 4, 1847, of scurvy
Born: May 3, 1817, Clifton, Glos., England

Turner, Hyrum (3 yrs.)
Son of Nelson and Lucynday Turner
Died: Mar. 27, 1847
Born: Feb. 28, 1844, Nauvoo, Ill.

Tuttle, Edward (55 yrs.)
Husband of Catherine Tuttle
Died: Aug. 17, 1847, of chills and fever
Born: July 1, 1792, Massachusetts

Tuttle, Luther (7 mos.)
Son of Ezeria and Ann Tuttle
Died: Aug. 13, 1847, of inflammation of bowels
Born: Dec. 22, 1846, Winter Quarters

Utley, Henry L. (7 yrs.)
Son of Samuel and Maria Utley
Died: Oct. 3, 1847, of canker and measles
Born: May 25, 1840, Perry County, Ala.

Utley, Jacob T. (9 yrs.)
Son of Samuel and Maria Utley
Died: Nov. 12, 1846, of dropsy and measles
Born: Dec. 3, 1837, Perry County, Ala.

Utley, Sarah E. (16 yrs.)
Daughter of Samuel and Maria Utley
Died: Nov. 16, 1847, of canker
Born: June 18, 1831, Perry County, Ala.

Utley, Maria (35 yrs.)
Wife of Samuel Utley
Died: Oct. 14, 1847, of canker
Born: Jan. 21, 1812, Chautague County, Tenn.

Uttley, James W. S. (14 yrs.)
Son of Samuel and Maria Uttley
Died: Nov. 5, 1847, of dropsy
Born: May 1, 1833, Perry County, Ala.

Vance, Lehi M. (27 days)
Son of John and Elizabeth Vance
Died: Oct. 9, 1846, of fever
Born: Sept. 12, 1846, Illinois

Van Velser, Henry G. (6 yrs.)
Son of Stephen and Fannie Van Velser
Died: May 17, 1847, of scurvy
Born: Jan. 20, 1841, New Rochelle, N.Y.

Wadsworth, Ann (36 yrs.)
No survivors given
Died: Oct. 6, 1846, of fever
Born: July 25, 1810, Salem, N.Y.

Wait, Rebecca (3 yrs.)
Daughter of John and Jane Wait
Died: Nov. 30, 1847, of canker
Born: Feb. 25, 1844, St. Louis, Mo.

Walker, Joseph E. (2 mos.)
Son of John and Elizabeth Walker
Died: Apr. 1, 1847, of cold
Born: Feb. 1, 1847, Winter Quarters

Weaks, Arvin (1 yr.)
Son of William and Caroline Weaks
Died: Apr. 18, 1847, of scurvy
Born: June 8, 1845, Nauvoo, Ill.

Welch, Nicholas (1 yr.)
Son of John and Elizabeth Welch
Died: Sept. 14, 1847, of canker
Born: Apr. 2, 1846, Nauvoo, Ill.

West, Alvy (51 yrs.)
Husband of Sally West
Died: Nov. 17, 1846, of fever
Born: June 21, 1795, Berkshire County, Ma.

West, Julia Ann (1 yr.)
Daughter of _____ and Sharlott Ameila West
Died: Aug. 16, 1847, of consumption
Born: Mar. 2, 1846, Nauvoo, Ill.

West, Sally (46 yrs.)
Wife of Alvy West
Died: Feb. 12, 1847
Born: Oct. 19, 1800, Onandaga County, N.Y.

Whitney, Doncerlos (age not given)
Son of Alonzo and Henryetty Whitney
Died: Nov. 27, 1846
Born: Warren County, Ohio

Whitney, Enoch K. (5 mos.)
Son of Lyman and Rhoda Ann Whitney
Died: Aug. 1, 1847, of inflammation of head
Born: Feb. 16, 1847, Winter Quarters

Whitney, Helen R. A.
Daughter of Horace and Helen Mar Whitney
Died: May 6, 1847, stillborn
Born: May 6, 1847, Winter Quarters

Willet, Elizabeth (2 yrs.)
Daughter of Jeremiah and Semanthy Willey
Died: Dec. 21, 1846, of canker
Born: July 20, 1844, Warsaw, Hancock County, Ill.

Williams, Helen Amilia (1 yr.)
Daughter of Gustavis and Maria Williams
Died: July 6, 1847, of congestive chills
Born: Dec. 31, 1845, Nauvoo, Ill.

Williams, John H. (6 yrs.)
Son of Peter and Elizabeth Williams
Died: Apr. 5, 1847
Born: Mar. 1, 1841, Manchester, England

Williams, Peter (35 yrs.)
Husband of Elizabeth Williams
Died: Oct. 22, 1846
Born: 1811, Cheshire, England

Woodruff, Ezra (3 days)
Son of Wilford and Phebe Woodruff
Died: Dec. 10, 1846
Born: Dec. 7, 1846, Winter Quarters

Woodruff, Joseph (1 yr.)
Son of Wilford and Phebe Woodruff
Died: Nov. 12, 1846, of canker
Born: July 14, 1845, Liverpool, England

Woodward, William S. (37 yrs.)
Husband of Mary C. Woodward
Died: Nov. 17, 1846, of chills and fever
Born: May 12, 1809, Upper Freehold, Monmouth County, N.J.

Wright, Enoch (18 days)
Son of Jonathan C. and Rebecca Wright
Died: Dec. 5, 1846, of spasms
Born: Nov. 16, 1846, at Winter Quarters

Young, Delinea Adalia (age not given)
Daughter of William and Adalia Young
Died: Nov. 28, 1846
Born: Winter Quarters

Young, Elizabeth (62 yrs.)
Wife of David Young
Died: Jan. 24, 1847, of dropsy
Born: Oct. 17, 1784, Tennessee

Young, Jane (27 yrs.)
Wife of George W. Young
Died: Feb. 14, 1847, of consumption
Born: May 21, 1819, Short Hills, Upper Canada

Young, Moroni (7 mos.)
Son of Brigham and Louisa Young
Died: Aug. 10, 1847, of teething and canker
Born: Jan. 8, 1847, Winter Quarters

Zabrisky, Mary Amanda Margaret (5 mos.)
Daughter of Louis and Mary Zabrisky
Died: July 9, 1847
Born: Jan. 17, 1847, Atkinson County, Mo.

Notes

Introduction

1. Florence Historical File.
2. Jenson, comp., "Manuscript History of Florence, Nebraska."
3. Journal of Hosea Stout, September 25, 1846.

Chapter One: A Beautiful and Delightful Situation

1. Olson, *History of Nebraska*, pp. 83-84.
2. Young, *Manuscript History, 1846-47*, Sept. 23, 1846.
3. Ibid., September 9, 1846.
4. Roberts, *A Comprehensive History of the Church of Jesus Christ of Latter-day Saints*, pp. 310-12.
5. Plat of Winter Quarters.
6. Pratt, *Autobiography*, pp. 342-43.
7. Journal of Anson Call.
8. Account book of Patty Sessions.
9. Kane, *The Mormons*, p. 92.

Chapter Two: Come to Zion

1. Carter, comp., *The Mormons from Ireland*, p. 3.
2. Pratt, *Autobiography*, p. 130.
3. Williams, comp., "Margaret Cowan Bryson."
4. Corbett, *Hyrum Smith, Patriarch*, p. 301.
5. Smith, *History of the Church* (HC) 7:198.
6. Daughters of the Utah Pioneers, *Mormon Emigration, 1840-1869*, p. 302.
7. HC 7:397-98.
8. Ibid., 7:439-40.
9. Ibid., 7:561-62.
10. Ibid., 7:566.
11. Journal of Joseph Fielding, pp. 90-96.
12. Young, *Manuscript History of Brigham Young, 1846-47*, pp. 374-75.
13. Journal of Thomas Bullock, Nov. 28, 1846.

Chapter Three: Why Should We Mourn?

1. Whitney, "Our Travels Beyond the Mississippi."
2. Young, *Manuscript History of Brigham Young*, pp. 33-34.
3. Clayton, *William Clayton's Journal*, p. 3.
4. Young, *Manuscript History*, p. 57.
5. Clayton, *Journal*, p. 3.

6. Young, *Manuscript History*, p. 57.
7. Ibid., pp. 52-54.
8. Young, *Manuscript History*, pp. 58-61.
9. Clayton, *Journal*, p. 3.
10. Diaries and account book of Patty Bartlett Sessions.
11. Young, *Manuscript History*, p. 258.
12. Sessions Family Group Sheets.
13. Clayton, *Journal*, p. 19.
14. Young, *Manuscript History*, p. 125.
15. *HC* 4:329-30.
16. Ibid., 7:325, 534-40.
17. Young, *Manuscript History*, pp. 148-49.
18. Cowley, *Wilford Woodruff, History of His Life and Labors*, p. 127.
19. Sonne, *Saints on the Seas*, pp. 148-49.
20. Cowley, *Wilford Woodruff*, p. 250.
21. Kimball, *Heber C. Kimball*, pp. 135-36.
22. Young, *Manuscript History*, p. 140.
23. Jenson, *LDS Biographical Encyclopedia* 1:357.
24. Pratt, *Autobiography*, p. 342.
25. Young, *Manuscript History*, p. 170.
26. Kimball, *Heber C. Kimball*, pp. 136-37.
27. Young, *Manuscript History*, p. 197.

CHAPTER FOUR: FIVE HUNDRED GOOD MEN

1. Young, *Manuscript History*, p. 222.
2. Pulsipher, "History in His Own Hand."
3. Tyler, *A Concise History of the Mormon Battalion*, pp. 343-44.
4. Pulsipher, "History in His Own Hand."
5. Tyler, *A Concise History of the Mormon Battalion*, p. 344.
6. Widtsoe, ed., *Discourses of Brigham Young*, pp. 476-79.
7. Young, *Manuscript History*, pp. 35, 40.
8. Morris, *Encyclopedia of American History*, pp. 209-10, 244.
9. Young, *Manuscript History*, pp. 35, 40.
10. Ibid., pp. 212-20.
11. Kane, *The Mormons*, p. 94.
12. *Hymns*, No. 55.
13. Cowley, *Wilford Woodruff*, p. 252.
14. Brooks, *John Doyle Lee*, pp. 95-105.
15. Young, *Manuscript History*, p. 262.
16. Ibid., p. 264.

CHAPTER FIVE: BUILDING A CITY

1. Young, *Manuscript History*, p. 268.
2. Ibid., pp. 268-88.
3. DeVoto, *The Year of Decision, 1846*, p. 48.
4. Young, *Manuscript History*, pp. 334-35.
5. Ibid., p. 378.
6. Ibid., p. 376.
7. Jenson, comp., "Manuscript History of Winter Quarters," September 11, 1846.
8. Plat of Winter Quarters.
9. Journal of Thomas Bullock, November 28, 1846.
10. Jenson, comp., "Manuscript History of Winter Quarters," November 7, 1846.
11. Journal of Hosea Stout, September 25, 1846.
12. Jenson, comp., "Manuscript History of Winter Quarters," November 7, 1846.
13. *Women's Exponent* 13:139.

14. Jenson, comp., "Manuscript History of Winter Quarters," November 12, 1846.
15. Noall, *Intimate Disciple*, p. 514.
16. Schindler, *Orrin Porter Rockwell*, p. 149.
17. Young, *Manuscript History*, p. 468.
18. Jenson, comp., "Historical Record," December 31, 1846.
19. Young, *Manuscript History*, p. 396; Roberts, *The Rise and Fall of Nauvoo*, pp. 360-68.
20. Young, *Manuscript History*, p. 409-21.
21. Ibid., p. 429.
22. Rogers, *Life Sketches*, pp. 35-42.
23. Young, *Manuscript History*, p. 435.
24. Ibid., p. 488.
25. *Journal of Discourses*, 6:173-4.
26. Young, *Manuscript History*, pp. 487-88.
27. *Journal of Discourses*, 8:354.
28. Young, *Manuscript History*, p. 297.
29. Ibid., p. 463.
30. Jenson, *LDS Biographical Encyclopedia*, 3:530.
31. D&C Sections 72, 124.
32. *HC* 5:120.
33. Young, *Manuscript History*, pp. 404, 425, 465.
34. Jenson, comp., "Manuscript History of Winter Quarters," November 26, 1846.
35. Account Book of Isaac Clark.
36. Stout, *On the Mormon Frontier*, 1:288.
37. Driggs, *The Old West Speaks*, pp. 98-99.
38. D&C Section 135.
39. Noall, *Intimate Disciple*, p. 514; Young, *Manuscript History*, pp. 503-5.

CHAPTER SIX: *AND SHOULD WE DIE*

1. Young, *Memoirs of a Utah Pioneer*, p. 4.
2. Kirby, "Burials at Winter Quarters."
3. Journal of Anson Call.
4. Turley, *The Theodore Turley Family Book*, pp. 50, 56, 57.
5. Faust, "The Refiner's Fire," *Ensign*, May, 1979, p. 4.
6. Woodruff, *Journals*, 3:93-97.
7. Noall, *Intimate Disciple*, p. 494.
8. Forsyth, "Life of Shadrach Roundy."
9. Jenson, comp., "Manuscript History of Winter Quarters," March 14, 1847.
10. *Women's Exponent*, 14:75.
11. Young, *Manuscript History*, p. 448.
12. Kirby, "Burials at Winter Quarters."
13. Young, *Manuscript History*, p. 538.
14. Jenson, comp., "Manuscript History of Winter Quarters," May 21, 1848; Jenson, *LDS Biographical Encyclopedia*, 3:713.

CHAPTER SEVEN: *WE'LL MAKE THE AIR WITH MUSIC RING*

1. McCune, "William Clayton," biographical preface to *William Clayton's Journal.*
2. Clayton, *William Clayton's Journal*, pp. 19-20.
3. *HC*, 7:333-35.
4. Jenson, *LDS Biographical Encyclopedia* 3:661.
5. *Journal of Discourses*, 15:341-54.
6. D&C 25:11-12.
7. *HC* 2:270.
8. Bowen, "The Versatile W. W. Phelps," p. 1.
9. D&C 55; 57:11-13.

10. Bowen, "The Versatile W. W. Phelps," pp. 51-53; *HC* 1:390.
11. *HC* 2:227.
12. Cornwall, *Stories of our Mormon Hymns*, pp. xxii-xxiv.
13. *HC* 410-28.
14. *HC* 4:142, 163.
15. Bowen, "The Versatile W. W. Phelps," pp. 131-38.
16. Jenson, *LDS Biographical Encyclopedia*, 3:392-95.
17. *Latter-day Saint Hymn Books*.
18. Young, *Manuscript History*, p. 6.
19. *Women's Exponent* 12:111.
20. Kane, *The Mormons*, pp. 30-31.
21. Jenson, comp., "Manuscript History of Winter Quarters," February 5, 1847.
22. Young, *Manuscript History*, p. 521.

CHAPTER EIGHT: *WE'LL FIND THE PLACE*

1. *HC* 5:85.
2. Affidavit of Anson Call.
3. *HC* 5:542-49.
4. Ibid., 5:479-81.
5. Ibid., 6:479-81.
6. Ibid., 7:401-37.
7. Young, *Manuscript History*, pp. 260, 290.
8. Pratt, *Autobiography*, pp. 345-46.
9. Young, *Manuscript History*, pp. 301-2.
10. *Collection of Sacred Hymns*.
11. Historical Plaque at Mount Pisgah Cemetery, Iowa.
12. Young, *Manuscript History*, p. 354.
13. Ibid., p. 370.
14. Ibid., pp. 298, 318.
15. DeVoto, *The Year of Decision, 1846*, pp. 43-46.
16. Young, *Manuscript History*, pp. 463-64.
17. Roberts, *A Comprehensive History of the Church*, 3:85.
18. Young, *Manuscript History*, pp. 463-64.
19. Ibid., p. 543.
20. Barron, *Orson Hyde*, pp. 177-78; Pratt, *Autobiography*, p. 358.
21. Jenson, *LDS Biographical Encyclopedia* (contains biographies of all 148 members of pioneer company), 4:693-725.
22. Spencer and Harmer, *Brigham Young at Home*, p. 74.
23. Jenson, *LDS Biographical Encyclopedia*, 4:703.
24. Patriarchal Blessing File.
25. Journal History of the Church, September 25, 1847.
26. Clayton, *Journal*, pp. 70-78, 143-52, 376.
27. Clayton, *The Latter-day Saints' Emigrants' Guide*.
28. *HC* 7:616-17.
29. Daughters of the Utah Pioneers, *Mormon Emigration, 1840-69*, pp. 254-56.
30. Young, *Manuscript History*, p. 564.
31. *HC* 7:621-23.

CHAPTER NINE: *SOME WHO STAYED*

1. Jenson, comp., "Manuscript History, Florence, Nebraska."
2. Ibid.
3. Hilton, "Joseph's Scattered Flock."
4. Fletcher, *Alpheus Cutler and the Church of Jesus Christ*, pp. 12-15.
5. *HC* 2:205.
6. Fletcher, *Alpheus Cutler*, p. 25.
7. D&C 118:4-5.

8. *HC*, 3:337-39.
9. D&C 124:132.
10. *HC* 6:629.
11. Fletcher, *Alpheus Cutler*, p. 41.
12. Young, *Manuscript History*, p. 302.
13. Jenson, comp., "Manuscript History of Winter Quarters," September 25, 1846.
14. Young, *Manuscript History*, pp. 415, 438.
15. Ibid., pp. 511, 536.
16. Flanders, "The Mormons Who Did Not Go West"; Cunningham, *The History of Manti*.
17. Fletcher, *Alpheus Cutler*, pp. 47-48.
18. Jenson, comp., "Historical Record," 1:227.
19. Kimball, *Heber C. Kimball*, pp. 129, 308.
20. Hilton, "Joseph's Scattered Flock"; Kimball, *Heber C. Kimball*, p. 308.
21. Miller, *Correspondence of George Miller with the Northern Islander*, p. 2.
22. D&C 124:20-23.
23. Miller, *Correspondence*, pp. 8-25.
24. *HC* 7:254-55, 261, 392, 628.
25. Miller, *Correspondence*, p. 31.
26. Pratt, *Autobiography*, pp. 341-42.
27. Miller, *Correspondence*, p. 36.
28. Wight, *An address by way of an abridged account*.
29. Young, *Manuscript History*, p. 545.
30. Miller, *Correspondence*, pp. 38-50.
31. *Deseret News Church Almanac*, 1982, p. 119.
32. Flanders, "The Mormons Who Did Not Go West."

CHAPTER TEN: WINTER QUARTERS REBORN

1. *HC* 7:623, 627-8.
2. Journal History of the Church, October 10, 1848.
3. Danker, "The Nebraska Winter Quarters Company and Florence," pp. 27-29.
4. Jenson, comp., "Manuscript History of Florence," March 22, 1856.
5. Danker. "The Nebraska Winter Quarters Company," p. 32.
6. Ibid., p. 36.
7. Jenson, *LDS Biographical Encyclopedia*, 1:627; Family Group Sheet, Alexander C. Pyper.
8. Danker, "The Nebraska Winter Quarters Company," p. 40.
9. Daughters of the Utah Pioneers, *Mormon Emigration 1842-69*, p. 263.
10. Journal of Wandle Mace.
11. *Millennial Star*, 18:637.
12. Sonne, *Saints on the Seas*, p. 57.
13. Ibid., p. 150.
14. Hafen, *Handcarts to Zion*, pp. 93-96, 192.
15. Daughters of the Utah Pioneers, *Mormon Emigration 1842-69*, p. 263.
16. Jenson, comp., "Manuscript History of Florence," April 4, 1856.
17. Ibid.; Hafen, *Handcarts to Zion*, pp. 145-48.
18. Jenson, comp., "Manuscript History of Florence," July 15, 1857.
19. *Conference Report*, April 1984; *Ensign*, May 1984, p. 81.
20. Journal of Wandle Mace, p. 178.
21. Danker, "The Nebraska Winter Quarters Company," p. 38.
22. Daughters of the Utah Pioneers, *Mormon Emigration, 1842-69*, pp. 264-65.
23. *Journal of Discourses*, 5:206.
24. Daughters of the Utah Pioneers, *Mormon Emigration, 1842-69*, pp. 266-67.
25. Hartley, Paper.
26. Jenson, *LDS Biographical Encyclopedia*, 1:361, 622, 806; 4:442, 500.
27. Danker, "The Nebraska Winter Quarters Company," p. 46.

BIBLIOGRAPHY

MANUSCRIPTS, DIARIES, JOURNALS

Bowen, Walter Deane. "The Versatile W. W. Phelps." Master's thesis, Brigham Young University, August, 1958.

Bullock, Thomas. Journal. Church Archives.

Call, Anson. Affidavit. Church Archives.

——. Journal. Owned by D. E. Hurst.

Clark, Isaac. Diary and Account Book. Church Archives.

Cunningham, R. E., comp. "The History of Manti." Church Archives.

Fielding, Joseph. Diary. Church Archives.

Flanders, Robert Bruce. "The Mormons Who Did Not Go West." Master's thesis, University of Wisconsin, 1954.

Florence Historical File. Florence Branch, Omaha Public Library, Omaha, Nebraska.

Forsyth, B. "Life of Shadrach Roundy." Term paper, Brigham Young University, n.d.

Hartley, William J. Paper presented before Mormon History Association, Omaha, Nebraska, 6 May 1983.

Hilton, Hope. "Joseph's Scattered Flock." Typescript, Brigham Young University Leadership Week, 1958.

Historical Plaque at Mount Pisgah Cemetery, Iowa.

Jenson, Andrew, comp. "Historical Record." Church Archives.

——. "Manuscript History of Florence, Nebraska." Church Archives.

——. "Manuscript History of Winter Quarters." Church Archives.

Journal History of the Church. Church Archives.

Kirby, Ethel B., comp. "Burials at Cutler's Park and Winter Quarters." Florence Historical File, Florence Branch, Omaha Public Library.

Mace, Wandle. Journal. Church Archives.

Patriarchal Blessing File. Church Archives.

Plat of Winter Quarters. State of Nebraska Archives, Lincoln, Nebraska, n.d.

Pulsipher and Alger Family Records. Owned by author.

Pulsipher, Zera. Autobiography. Church Archives.

——. "History in His Own Hand." Church Archives.

Sessions Family Group Sheets. Genealogy Library, The Church of Jesus Christ of Latter-day Saints.

Sessions, Patty Bartlett. Account Book. Church Archives.

———. Diary. Church Archives.

Stout, Hosea. Journal. Church Archives.

Whipple, Nelson Wheeler. Memoirs. Church Archives.

Williams, Janet J., comp. "Margaret Cowan Bryson." Typescript owned by author.

PUBLISHED SOURCES

Barron, Howard H. *Orson Hyde, Missionary, Apostle, Colonizer.* Bountiful, Utah: Horizon Publishers, 1977.

Brooks, Juanita. *John Doyle Lee, Zealot, Pioneer, Builder, Scapegoat.* Glendale, California: Arthur H. Clark, 1961.

Brown, Joseph E. *The Mormon Trek West.* Garden City, N.Y.: Doubleday, 1980.

Carter, Kate B., comp. *The Mormons from Ireland.* Salt Lake City: Daughters of the Utah Pioneers, 1970.

Clayton, William. *The Latter-day Saints' Emigrants' Guide.* St. Louis: Chambers and Knapp, 1848.

———. *William Clayton's Journal.* Salt Lake City: Deseret News, 1921.

Collection of Sacred Hymns for the Church of the Latter-day Saints: Selected by Emma Smith. Kirtland: F. G. Williams and Co., 1835.

Corbett, Don C. *Mary Fielding Smith, Daughter of Zion.* Salt Lake City: Deseret Book, 1966.

Corbett, Pearson H. *Hyrum Smith, Patriarch.* Salt Lake City: Deseret Book, 1963.

Cornwall, J. Spencer. *Stories of our Mormon Hymns.* Salt Lake City: Deseret Book, 1963.

Cowley, Mathias F. *Wilford Woodruff, History of His Life and Labors.* Salt Lake City: Bookcraft, 1964.

Danker, Donald F. "The Nebraska Winter Quarters Company and Florence." *Nebraska History* 37:27, March, 1956.

Daughters of the Utah Pioneers. *Mormon Emigration, 1840-69.* Salt Lake City: Daughters of the Utah Pioneers, January 1963.

———. *Thomas L. Kane and the Mormons.* Salt Lake City: Daughters of the Utah Pioneers, October 1956.

Deseret News. Salt Lake City, Utah.

Deseret News 1985 Church Almanac. Salt Lake City: Deseret News, 1985.

DeVoto, Bernard. *The Year of Decision, 1846.* Boston: Little Brown, 1943.

Doctrine and Covenants. Salt Lake City: The Church of Jesus Christ of Latter-day Saints.

Driggs, Howard R. *The Old West Speaks.* New York: Bonanza Books, 1956.

Ensign. Salt Lake City: The Church of Jesus Christ of Latter-day Saints.

Fletcher, Rupert J., and Daisy W. Fletcher. *Alpheus Cutler and the Church of Jesus Christ.* Independence, Missouri: The Church of Jesus Christ, 1974.

Hafen, LeRoy R., and Anne W. Hafen. *Handcarts to Zion, 1856-60.* Glendale: Arthur H. Clark Co., 1976.

Holy Bible (King James Version).

Hymns. Salt Lake City: The Church of Jesus Christ of Latter-day Saints, 1948.

Jenson, Andrew W. *LDS Biographical Encyclopedia.* 4 vols. Salt Lake City: Andrew Jenson History Company, 1901.

Journal of Discourses. 26 vols. London: Latter-day Book Depot, 1854-1886.

Kane, Thomas L. *The Mormons.* Philadelphia: King and Baird, 1850.

Kimball, Stanley B. *Heber C. Kimball, Mormon Patriarch and Pioneer.* Urbana: University of Illinois Press, 1981.

Latter-day Saint Hymn Books, all editions. Microfilm, Church Archives.

Miller, George. *Correspondence of George Miller with the Northern Islander, 1855.* Church Archives.

Millennial Star (Liverpool, England). 1840-present.

Morris, Richard B. *Encyclopedia of American History.* New York: Harper and Rowe, 1953.

Nebraska History (Lincoln, Nebraska). 1956.

Noall, Claire. *Intimate Disciple, A Portrait of Willard Richards.* Salt Lake City: University of Utah Press, 1957.

Olsen, James C. *History of Nebraska.* Lincoln: University of Nebraska Press, 1951.

Pratt, Parley P. *Autobiography of Parley P. Pratt.* Salt Lake City: Deseret Book, 1979.

Roberts, Brigham H. *A Comprehensive History of The Church of Jesus Christ of Latter-day Saints.* 6 vols. Provo, Utah: Brigham Young University Press, 1965.

——. *The Life of John Taylor.* Salt Lake City: Bookcraft, 1963.

——. *The Missouri Persecutions.* Salt Lake City: Bookcraft, 1965.

——. *The Rise and Fall of Nauvoo.* Salt Lake City: Bookcraft, 1965.

Rogers, Aurelia Spencer. *Life Sketches.* Salt Lake City: George Q. Cannon and Sons, 1898.

Schindler, Harold. *Orrin Porter Rockwell, Man of God, Son of Thunder.* Salt Lake City: University of Utah Press, 1983.

Smith, Joseph. *History of the Church of Jesus Christ of Latter-day Saints.* 7 vols. Edited by B. H. Roberts. Salt Lake City: The Church of Jesus Christ of Latter-day Saints, 1932-51.

Sonne, Coway B. *Saints on the Seas, A Maritime History of Mormon Migration, 1830-1890.* Salt Lake City: University of Utah Press, 1983.

Spencer, Clarissa Young, with Mabel Harmer. *Brigham Young at Home.* Salt Lake City: Deseret Book, 1963.

Stout, Hosea. *On the Mormon Frontier, the Diary of Hosea Stout.* 2 vols. Salt Lake City: University of Utah Press, 1964.

Turley, Nancy Romans. *The Theodore Turley Family Book.* Privately printed, 1977.

Tyler, Daniel Watts. *A Concise History of the Mormon Battalion in the Mexican War.* Chicago: Rio Grande Press, 1881.

Whitney, Helen Mar. "Our Travels Beyond the Mississippi." *Women's Exponent* 12:26, 82, 90.

Widtsoe, John A., comp. *Discourses of Brigham Young.* Salt Lake City: Deseret Book, 1954.

Wight, Lyman. *An address by way of an abridged account.* Church Archives.

Woman's Exponent (Salt Lake City). 1884-1885.

Woodruff, Wilford. *Journals of Wilford Woodruff.* 4 vols. Typescript, Midvale, Utah: Signature Books, 1983.

Young, Brigham. *Manuscript History of Brigham Young, 1846-47.* Salt Lake City: Eldon J. Watson, 1971.

Young, John R. *Memoirs of a Utah Pioneer, 1847.* Salt Lake City: Deseret News, 1920.

INDEX